tell 'em

the story of a girl whose first
language was not the spoken word

Liysa Callsen

*For my girls,
be everything!*

Your support, patience and amazing spirit
make me a better person.

This is a memoir. It reflects the author's present recollection of her experiences over a period of years. The names of some people and their identifying characteristics have been changed.

Printed in the United States of America
First Edition

Published by The Cottage Corollary
Two Rivers, WI

Cover and book design by Laura Wiegert

ISBN: 978-0-9823792-1-9

www.codadiva.com

. . . the programming you picked up in childhood,
you are responsible for fixing.

- Ken Keyes, Jr.

CONTENTS

ACKNOWLEDGMENTS

The journey I took when writing a memoir was not only time consuming, but emotion consuming. There were so many people who supported me in one way or another, cumulatively making this a success.

Thanks to everyone who took a moment to listen to me babble about a paragraph, concept, or emotion. Thanks to Cindy Torstenson and Sue Fink for allowing me to talk it out. Thanks to Lisa Warsinske, Leah O'Barski and Jennifer Rada for allowing a deeper connection by helping me see my gifts with laughter and reflections. Thanks to Syllviea Hagen and Astrid Stromberg for their virtual insight. Thanks to Bobbi Jo, John, Riley, and Mackenzie Johnson along with Cathy, Jason, and Matilda Newport for inviting the girls to play, many times.

Thanks to my CODA (Children of Deaf Adults) friends, Barbara Derengowski for being my biggest cheerleader in the early CODA stages and in memory of Diana Nelson, her tenacity continues to inspire me. To all the other CODAs I have met and have yet to meet, my deepest respect for the culture we share.

Thanks to those who love the arts, including Lisa Golda for her encouragement and platform to perform my first one-woman show, resulting in a significant turning point in my life. Thanks especially to Ron Kaminski for giving me my first acting role in The Vagina Monologues, in which I met Kathryn Gahl. Without Kathryn, an accomplished writer, this book would not have been written. Her vision, persistence, and constant coaching—plus the writing alcove she and Robert provided me in their home—brought this book to life.

Thank you to the early readers. With your insight and feedback the book became an even more intense journey for the reader as well as myself; Crystal J. Casavant-Otto, Mary Jo and Jim Hoftiezer, Gregg Novachek, Tim and Karen Schroeder, Jessica Lyn Van Slooten, Dixie Zittlow, and Jeff and Mari Dawson.

A great gratitude to Tim Schroeder and his countless hours spent improving punctuation and my bilingual, grammatical style.

Thanks to the Kickstarter backers who support this project; Marie Dimond, Pam Walker, Crystal Casavant-Otto, Astrid Stromberg, Maureen Mould, Brenda and John Fredrick, Valerie Krejcie, Mary Ann Denson, Laura Wiegert, Laurie and Kevin Crawford, Karin Conway, Bobbi Jo Johnson, Amy Luczak, Cindi Ashbeck, Jennie and Scott Littrell, Becky and John Swain, Missy, Erik Witteborg lml/, Dave Saims, Stacy and Marco Coppola, Leah and Wayne O'Barski, Jennifer Rada, Kerry Trask, and Robert Gahl.

Special thanks to Laura Wiegert for the design of this book. I'm so in love with it. Thank you Shirley Cleereman for assisting me through the publishing world with your knowledge.

Thanks to my longtime friends Colleen Mora, Janine Fitzgibbons, Kim D'Arcy and Missy Smedley, for the unconditional love for so many years. Also, to my extended childhood families; Emery and Suzanne Price and Kathy and John Valentine.

Thanks to my family for their individual showing of support. To my parents, Joan and David Croll for giving me a beautiful language and culture that I cherish; my in-laws, Avid and Patricia Callsen for the acceptance and love they provide; my brother Marty, I'm enjoying our childhood stories as we pass them down to our children together; my sister-in-law Casi, for being just rockin' cool; and my step-son, Randall, for helping out babysitting during the writing times – I write in hopes that one day you will understand.

And once again, many thanks to Kathryn Gahl, first a friend, then an editor and now a family member. Without her amazing dedication, sacrifice, and support, this book would not have happened. Thank you, Kathryn, for believing in my story before I did.

Finally, thanks to Carl, the man I always knew was connected to my soul. Thanks for your support, understanding, and love through one of the biggest growth times of my life.

FOREWORD

One afternoon, an insurance salesman made a call to our Detroit home. I was ten. I remember sitting in our kitchen at the round table. I was seated with my Deaf parents on either side of me. It was as if I was the top of the pyramid. My role was to facilitate communication in a way where both of them could see me at the same time.

Back then, I would not have been able to explain how American Sign Language (ASL) is a visual language. What that means is this: the translation of English to ASL flows through the interpreter's hands and body to make word pictures. These "pictures" convey images and concepts rather than utterances word-for-word. Without knowing this philosophical difference, I simply did what was expected of me. I interpreted.

My parents were seated so both could see me to understand what I was conveying. I looked at the insurance guy, who seemed to be a young professional. He was probably in his thirties. He didn't sit down; he stood across from me. From where I sat and because I was short, I was looking up at him through our kitchen table light fixture. I couldn't really see him too well. He made me nervous. As my parents were given the paperwork, the young man looked at me and said, "Tell 'em I'll be explaining some definitions." He then went on to talk about premiums, long-term disability and beneficiaries. I was overwhelmed on the inside but I managed to keep up. The meeting happened, my parents got life insurance. I can't say for sure that I helped much.

For me, growing up with Deaf parents, it was just another day.

Deaf

—

RESPONSIBILITY

As a child, interpreting was one of my chores. This led to some complex situations. In 1985, Mom had a series of doctor appointments to find out what was behind her incredibly painful headaches. She had been referred to several different kinds of doctors. There weren't many interpreters available, so I dutifully went with Mom to all of these appointments.

One winter morning, Mom and I got up before the sun rose. With my eyes heavy with sleep, I fumbled through my closet and dresser drawers. I put on a pair of my dark blue Jordache jeans. I was so cold; I shivered as I pulled on my long purple knit sweater. It came to my thighs and covered my butt. To ensure I'd be warm, I wore my purple and white striped leg warmers. I didn't bother brushing my hair. I heard Mom shuffling around the kitchen and now making her way down the hall to my room. She came back to check on me, most likely wondering if I had gotten dressed yet.

"Ready?" she signed. I barely nodded and then followed Mom. We got into the car as the sun started to break through the sky. She had an appointment at the University of Michigan Hospital in Ann Arbor. It was a half an hour drive.

When we arrived, I realized why we had to leave early. It was an enormous hospital. The hallway could have housed an entire auto dealership and seemed to stretch for miles. We walked the halls a long time before we finally reached the correct waiting room. The waiting room was different, innovative before its time. It reminded me of a hotel lobby. It was an open space with sofas and comfy chairs. Beautiful coffee tables set the stage for conversation areas. I had never seen anything like it.

All the waiting rooms we had waited in before were small. Usually a handful of chairs outlined the perimeter of the waiting room. Sometimes there was a small steel end table shoved in the corner, supporting an outdated ceramic lamp that took up the table.

Mom and I took our seats in the fancy waiting room and my mind drifted to what I knew about my mother.

She had short, black hair, starting to turn grey. She went back and forth between leaving it grey and dying it auburn in our kitchen sink. Mom loved that rich color and pronounced it "awbern." Mom was about five foot five with olive skin that tanned easily in the summer. Her skin was always super smooth and soft—a quality that came to comfort me during times of stress. She loved lemons. She would eat them like an orange, biting right into them and peeling them off the rind. She loved them so much that her front teeth eventually curled and she required caps to fix them. Mom also loved to paint. She was in a painting circle, a group of Deaf women met monthly. Each month a new project was taught by the host. They painted lamp bases, frames and wreaths. My mom was also skilled in sewing. She sewed quilts and pillows.

I came back to the task at hand, realizing that no matter what waiting room Mom and I were in, I treasured this time, when Mom and I had time to chat. Sometimes we talked about nothing in particular, small talk or things happening around us. Other times we talked about crafts and school. We also talked about our friends, both mine and hers. Now that I think about it, it's interesting how detailed we explained our lives with our respective set of friends. Of course, as a mom, she knew my friends. And, I knew her friends very well. I knew about their families and jobs. Mom shared with me the bond she had with these people as if she was talking to a girlfriend.

I cherished talking to Mom. It was partly talking to her, but also seeing myself sign. I loved ASL so much. Some hearing people "love to hear themselves talk;" well, I was a girl who "loved to see herself sign." Just as dancers practiced in the mirror, I practiced signing in the mirror. I appreciated the beauty and lyrical movement of each sign.

The nurse called us into the doctor's office. When the doctor arrived, everything seemed to be as it should. A standard appointment designed to find the cause of my mother's headaches. However, I felt a shift in the tension. My mother was prepared. She had her notes to help her answer questions like the frequency of the headaches, degree of pain, and any triggers. However, the doctor's first question was, "How's your memory?"

Mom didn't anticipate this question. She rushed to answer, "Fine," adding a confident head nod as she spoke.

I could tell she thought the question was odd by her facial expressions. The doctor asked a second question about her behavior and moods. Mom became confused and visibly upset.

Mom asked, "What kind of doctor are you?" When the response was psychiatrist, my mother had a fit.

When I relived this memory, I shared it with Mom last year.

She said, "Do you remember what I did?"

I didn't.

She told me that she had jumped up and given a few choice words that probably sounded like growls and groans to the doctors. She grabbed me by the arm, said, "Let's go," and stormed out of the office. She was upset by the thought that she needed psychiatric treatment.

Looking back on that now, I wonder why I didn't remember Mom's assertiveness. I can only conclude that because I didn't have to translate it, I didn't retain it. Many times, Mom would ask me to help her re-count or re-explain an earlier appointment. Sometimes I helped further by giving analogies or explaining some of the words and breaking it down with real-life examples.

A few weeks after Mom stormed out of the University hospital, she returned back to her primary doctor. She was no longer angry. It was time to finally diagnose the problem. This time Mom and I were shown into a small room. As a twelve year old, I felt the coldness of this room. It was not an office, and it did not house any equipment or tools. There was a small desk mounted to the wall, with three drawers. The top of the desk was cleared off. Over the desk on the wall was the x-ray light. It looked like one of those old medicine cabinets that slid from either direction. There was a chair that matched the desk. Mom was shown a chair to sit in. There wasn't a place for me until the doctor left the room and returned with a rolling stool. I sat with my back to the door in this tiny room while the doctor sat in his chair and Mom in hers.

I was again the top of the pyramid.

The doctor sat down, grabbed the chart. His head faced down at the desk. He began to speak with a very heavy Indian accent without making eye contact.

Mom noticed his mouth moving and turned to me.

I tilted my head over in his direction.

Mom was waiting.

I leaned a bit closer. Nothing sounded intelligible to my twelve-year old self.

The doctor continued. I squinted.

Mom looked from the doctor to me.

I heard the word "Tests." I faced Mom, nodded, and signed, "Tests."

The doctor flipped some pages.

I waited.

Mom waited.

The doctor said, "Found."

I turned my eyes and hands to Mom. "Tests. Finished. Found."

Mom's body leaned forward.

The doctor continued.

I heard, "Results."

I sat sternly as I delivered the results to Mom.

There was a moment of silence.

I heard, "Operate."

Multiple lines creased my forehead.

Mom turned her eyes to me.

The doctor's words pierced my ears.

I froze.

The doctor stopped talking, looked up at my mother.

My mother's face told the doctor she was waiting.

The doctor looked at me.

My hands were in mid air. I hadn't found the right signs yet.

He looked me in the eyes.

"Tell her," he paused.

I moved my head slowly to look into his eyes, thinking, was I really going to have to tell her? The sign for "tell her" is placing an index finger at the chin and then moving it to point towards the person spoken to.

He spoke slower and stretched his pronunciation of each syllable.

"Tell her, she will need to have brain surgery."

My heart sunk.

Seconds passed. My mother signed, "What say?"

My eyes burned. The sign she used for "what say" was placing the index finger at the chin, tapping it a few times as if to receive what was being spoken.

Again, my mother signed, "What say?"

I turned to face her. I wished I could run away.

I pointed to the doctor and spoke verbally, "HE. . ."

I continued to sign but now without my voice, "SAY. . ."

With my index finger on my own chin, I moved it towards Mom. It felt like I was pointing a loaded gun aimed directly at her.

The doctor nodded to me, go on.

I forced a swallow and continued, "You. Must. Surgery. On. Brain."

The sign for surgery, a fist with an extended thumb. The thumb motioned to "cut." In this case, I had my thumb cutting my forehead.

I dropped my hands to my sides.

My mother heaved a sigh and held her forehead in her hands.

I was twelve. Twelve, not even a teenager yet. What was this doctor thinking, giving a child this kind of responsibility? What was my mother thinking giving her daughter this kind of responsibility? What was I thinking? Probably, just another day.

As usual within these settings, I was calm on the outside, but inside I was scared. I was scared and worried. I wanted to ask Mom what it all meant. But I knew she didn't know because I was the one telling her. I wanted someone to be prepared with the information and inform me, hopefully with some thought as to how to soothe my fears. I wanted Mom to hug me. I wanted someone to realize that they had just relied on a child to tell their mother—you are going to have surgery.

I didn't ask for a hug. Mom looked worried and I felt I had to be strong. I didn't have any questions for the Doctor, but I did for Mom. I wanted to ask her, what does he mean—surgery?

After a few moments, I found out what would be involved in the procedure. I had to explain where the incision would be, explain that a staple would be inserted and then detailed recovery expectations.

We went home. Nothing more was said about it. On the day of the surgery, I went to school. I wondered why I wasn't needed to help translate. Did Mom send me to school because she realized the seriousness of the situation? Perhaps she thought if there were complications, it would be in my best interest not to be there.

Around the time Mom was probably being prepped for surgery, I stared at the clock in history class. It was 8:10 a.m. I wanted to be at the hospital. I kept thinking, how could she be getting along without me? Was she being told the right things? I didn't want the responsibilities and yet, I craved them because I wanted to ensure that Mom was alright. I had already been there each step of the way on the diagnosis, so now I felt left out.

As it turned out, Mom had a blood clot in several veins in the front part of the brain. It had been there since birth. Mom recovered well. When she was brought home from the hospital, her face was bruised and her hair had been shaved. She settled into her bed to rest. I gave her a gentle hug and my cheek brushed lightly against hers. Her exceptionally soft skin on mine allowed me to exhale a sigh of relief.

This type of responsibility became a component to my life. Although I didn't know it at the time, the translating would shape me. It actually started when I was in the first grade, helping Dad with phone calls. When I arrived home from school, he'd have a list of calls for me. I'd go to my position by the rotary telephone. I'd lift the receiver with one hand and with my other hand, my index finger found the large circles placed over the numbers one through zero. I found the first number and forced it forward as far as it could go to the stopper. It needed to reach the end to be registered. Sometimes my small fingers slipped slightly in the big holes, causing the number not to fully retract to its original space in a smooth manner. I was forced to start over.

While I made the phone calls, Dad sat at the kitchen table. We were only a foot away from each other. He was a tall man and when he was seated still looked tall. He had dull wavy brown hair. It had a distinct smell, a smell of sandalwood from the brush he used every morning to push his curls from side to side. His hair was always short. I'm sure he must have had it cut, but I never remember it needing to be. In fact, I don't ever remember going with him for a haircut. At my age, I went with him for many other things, though.

Dad mostly wore his navy or dark khaki pants. Around the house he had on his white V-neck T-shirt tucked into his pants and finished off with a belt. When he went out, he'd put on a plaid short-sleeved shirt. His shirts always had a breast pocket. This was where he kept a small note pad along with his pens and pencils. He had at least three writing utensils at all times. When out in the hearing world, if he needed to write something down, there was no fumbling and asking the hearing person for paper. He was equipped.

As I dialed and listened to the phone ringing on the other end, Dad was already giving me information for the call. I raised my index finger and extended my arm in his direction with a fast and stiff movement which meant, wait, I'm not ready.

"Not. Answer," I explained.

Dad's shoulders slouched as he relaxed in his chair.

The ringing stopped. A woman answered, "Hello, Dr. Smith's office."

"Hi, my Dad wants to make an appointment."

Click.

The receptionist hung up.

I turned to Dad and signed, "She hung up." I showed him by using my hand, signing "telephone" with the thumb and pinky finger extended while the remaining fingers were folded in my palm. I placed the thumb of my "hand telephone," at my ear and the pinky finger at my mouth. I moved my hand from my ear into the opened palm of my other hand to say, click.

Dad asked me to dial again.

I again dialed the number and as the phone rang, I faced Dad and counted with my fingers, one. . . two. . . the line picked up. I immediately dropped my hand and straightened up. My eyes were pulled from my father's gaze as if the voice on the other end commanded my attention. Dad sensed the phone was answered and would immediately sign, "Tell 'em. I. Want. Make. Appointment."

This time, I said, "Hi, I'm calling for my Dad," hoping to buy time, to explain why a child was calling. Again, the receptionist hung up. I wanted to earn the respect of Dad for doing a good job. I was adamant to master this phone call. I soon realized I had to sound more grown up. I realized I had to have more power in my voice. So, I chose to enunciate clearer and slower.

After three failed attempts, Dad and I gave up.

Sometimes I felt disappointed that I wasn't able to help Dad; other times it was an inconvenience and I would rather be watching TV. Besides, that's what my brother Marty was doing.

Marty was a cute boy who held onto his baby-fat for a bit longer than most. His hair was reddish brown and he had freckles. During my early elementary years, I was never allowed to go any place unless I brought my brother. I felt like he was a millstone around my neck. I just wanted my own time. He had to come with me everywhere I went. When the neighborhood kids would walk up to Stroh's Ice Cream parlor 14 blocks away, I had to take Marty.

Years later, when Marty made his own friends, I never got invited. I felt animosity towards him. I also remembered thinking it was really unfair. Mom and Dad didn't force him to include me.

When Marty would sign to Mom and Dad, he would sign sloppy or lazy. I would immediately jump in to clean it up. The placement of his hands was limp, instead of sturdy; it could have been considered a slur or grunt in English. Without being asked, I would correct or take over the conversation to let Mom and Dad know I was there to help. It felt second nature to me. Besides, the approval I got from Mom and Dad made me feel fulfilled.

When the phone rang in my house, I would leap from wherever I was to answer it. It was an unwritten rule that I would be answering the phone first. The rotary phone was located on top of the TTY. A TTY (Text Telephone Device) was a gigantic machine. It was a three foot-high by four-foot wide typewriter. It had a built-in shelf just for the telephone. It looked like it had been designed for the Army, painted a deep forest green. It was big, clunky and ugly. The true purpose of the machine was for my parents to communicate with their friends.

I generally answered the phone by the second ring. "Hello." I'd say. No answer. I'd try one more time just to be sure, "Hello." If it was quiet on the other end or I heard background noises, I knew it was for Mom or Dad. I then flipped the switch on the TTY to "on." I placed the phone handle on the adapter; suction cups kept the phone in place at the ear and mouth pieces.

I typed, "HELLO GA." GA was short-hand that meant Go Ahead and indicated it was their turn to reply. Morse code sounds transmitted over phone lines punched out the letters.

I loved the sound the machine made. When it was turned on, the hum of the machine brought it to life. It also turned on a light bulb inside which illuminated the paper where words formed. Soon, the outside world would be sending their messages. When the caller responded, HELLO THIS IS ANNE GA, the TTY became magic. Letter by letter, the typebars flew from their position underneath the hood of the machine and landed on the paper. The typebars were heavy and each letter shook the large machine, cha-chunk. The longer the sentence, the more the machine thumped. The more it thumped, the more it made the floor tremble. The machine only typed in capital letters. I would walk over to Mom and sign, "phone." She would go over to the TTY and sit down to chat with the other caller.

When the TTY was not being used, I played on it. My fingers felt cozy in the large round keys. The keys were tall and smooth. The tops were slightly indented as if intended for my fingertips to fit snugly on them. As I typed my name, each letter cha-chunked. The letter L pulled from its position and landed on the paper. I timed my movements slowly at first, but then I would increase the rhythm. Faster and faster my fingers stroked the keys until I ultimately scrambled my fingers across the keyboard. This would send the typebars flying simultaneously and entangle them. I stood to fix the mess, holding onto the side of the TTY. I found the button that released the top cover and opened it toward the wall. It was simple to fix. We had our first TTY for about 15 years. The next TTY was much smaller. It looked like a small typewriter. The new roll-top desk Mom bought replaced the huge monstrosity TTY and then the smaller TTY fit inside the desk.

Years later, when I was 21, I spotted several TTYs in the Smithsonian Museum. As I entered the room filled with NASA memorabilia, there were half a dozen models lined up in a row. My eyes bulged out and I felt confused and bewildered. I was so surprised to see these machines in such a prestigious museum. As I walked over to take a closer look at them, I thought it was an illusion. How could our TTY be there? In the Smithsonian. There were no chairs at the machine, so I semi-hunched over the keyboard. I put my hands in first typing position and closed my eyes. As I gently glided my fingers over the very familiar chunky keyboard and spelled out my name. I gently tapped the keys, careful not to press them down. HELLO MOM DAD. I typed my thoughts as they came to me. THIS IS UNBELIEVEABLE. I HAD ONE OF THESE. I stopped. With eyes still closed, I brought my fingers back to first position. I paused and drifted back to my childhood. A smile started to form on my face as I remembered pounding on these round large keys.

Suddenly, I was nine and typing as fast as I could. I heard the machine cha-chunk all over again and saw the typebars get tangled up inside the machine. As I slowly opened my eyes, I couldn't help but remember how these were in Deaf people's homes. I had had no idea TTYs were conceived from the technology that was used by NASA and were now a part of history.

(QUESTIONS

When I told people my parents were Deaf, the same three questions were always asked:

Both of them?

Why aren't you deaf?

How did you learn to talk?

Sometimes *both of them* was more a statement than a question. Nine out of ten people responded with shock. The other one out of ten were awed. I watched as their brains personalized what it would be like not to hear, unable to fathom how they would function if deaf. They were hearing-dependent; some have told me they would rather be blind. When they discovered both of my parents were deaf, their jaws dropped. I never understood why it was more shocking to learn both of my parents were deaf.

After their shock was over, they started to wonder *why aren't you deaf?* I think their rationale was that, you already shocked me with two people being deaf, so now explain why aren't you deaf. My condensed answer was, it's not hereditary. This is fact: 90% of deaf children are born to hearing adults and 90% of deaf parents have hearing children. So, hereditary deafness correlates to about 10% of deaf parents have deaf children.

In my family, deafness is not genetic and both of my parents are the only Deaf people in their families. You may have noticed I capitalized the d in Deaf. I've learned that a capital D in Deaf applied to someone who could not hear, used sign language, and recognized they were part of a Deaf community. When the d is not capitalized, for me, it meant simply a hearing loss, like when grandparents gradually lose their hearing, and become deaf. While I can hear, I still feel Deaf at times because of my want to be connected to the community.

My father David Croll was born deaf as a result of my grandmother having the measles while pregnant. David was born in 1939, two years before the end of the depression. It was the same year the United States declared its neutrality in the European war when Germany invaded Poland, effectively beginning World War II. In Germany, Hitler announced to rid the land of "useless eaters" and ordered the deaf and disabled to be killed. Estimates reported around 2,000 deaf babies were taken and killed by lethal injection or starvation. Mothers were told their babies died from natural causes.

Back in the United States, within the Deaf world, Gallaudet College was celebrating its 75th anniversary of providing college education for Deaf students.

My father's parents were Samuel and Gladys Croll, from Detroit, Michigan. Grandpa Sam was one of six children. Born in Canada, his parents came from a *shetetl* in Russia's Pale of Settlement. A shetetl was typically a small town with a large Jewish population that existed in Central and Eastern Europe until the Holocaust.

Grandpa Sam became a dentist and had his own practice in Detroit. He died in 1981 when I was nine. I remember his kind demeanor, captured in every photo I have of him. He was soft spoken and never raised his voice. His eyes always twinkled with love but I sensed a glimmer of sadness when he smiled. When he died at the age of 76, I kept thinking he was so young, and I had wanted more time to get to know him.

Grandmother Gladys Croll was born and raised in Toronto, Canada. She was one of four children. She also grew up in a Jewish family. Grandma's background was in social work and she stopped working to raise a family. I didn't know much about Grandma's family, she only spoke about her sister.

During the time my grandparents were expecting a baby, another couple in the family was also expecting. Within a week, two babies were welcomed into the Croll family.

I can only imagine how it may have gone when the news of my father's disability was delivered. Grandmother was resting in her hospital room, painted drab and bland. Only portions of the morning sun illuminated the room because the windows hadn't been cleaned for some time. The doctor, quiet and reserved, walked into the room. His head was down, a sign that something was wrong.

Samuel got up from his chair to be with Gladys at her bedside.

The doctor pressed his lips together, paused and then spoke. At his hesitation, Gladys and Samuel emotionally braced themselves.

"I'm afraid I have some horrible news," the doctor began.

The sound of the doctor's voice surely increased their heartbeats and rattled their nerves.

"Your son, he's deaf." The doctor hung his head lower.

Seconds passed into what must have seemed like hours. Silence filled the room.

What mixed emotions did Gladys and Samuel feel at that time? What could have been the first thing they thought of individually? Who would have spoken first?

Perhaps it was my grandmother who said, "Are you sure?" or, "How can you tell?" or, "Let's do a re-test!"

Or was it my grandfather who said, "What can we do about it?" or, "How can we fix it?" or, "What's the next step?"

"I'm sorry, your baby cannot hear, he's deaf and dumb." The doctor added an insult.

Now, within minutes of being shocked about their bundle of joy's deafness, the doctor just called their baby dumb. Had Gladys and Samuel ever heard that term before? If so, did their minds rush to the time they first heard it, connecting that image to their newborn?

It was a term used in the thirties. It was meant to describe being mute. However, the word alone implied only what it could—dumb.

I shudder to think that halfway across the world, during a time of war, Hitler was ordering deaf babies killed.

Gladys and Samuel now entered their own war. They were discharged from the hospital to fight without resources, information or support.

My father had been born six days after his cousin. The news of a different baby, a healthy baby, within the family was fresh in Gladys's mind.

My grandmother must have felt jealous. Two births so close to each other, a healthy baby and her deaf-and-dumb baby.

Once back at home, Grandpa returned to work. Now, Grandma was on her own on how to care for her first child, aggravated by the fact that her child was deaf. I can only imagine the internal voices that screamed at my grandmother all day long as she fumbled about as new mothers do.

The pressure mounted as she compared herself to her sister-in-law's experience. What would it be like to have a hearing child? The example was right in front of her.

She most likely compared the cousins growing up at every stage of their lives, the hearing child's life full of opportunity, while she was left with no direction on how to fill a deaf child's life with joy. Denial turned to anger and anger brought resentment.

While World War II was building momentum, another war built inside my grandmother.

Family lore told that Gladys lashed out during this very stressful time. She called her sister-in-law. After a couple of rings, the phone was answered with "Hello," in what must have sounded like singsong from the new mother.

"*You* should have had the deaf baby!" My grandmother shouted. A sharp loud statement formed in the back of her throat and from the bottom of her heart, she added, ". . . not me!"

Gladys and Samuel seldom used sign language in the home. There were some home signs, made-up gestures to identify daily needs. Grandma knew the ASL alphabet. She would often just form the first letter of the word as she mouthed the rest of the word. It was faster than signing each letter.

My grandparents were able to provide the best education for David. They discovered a school in St. Louis that specialized in education for deaf students. It was an oral school promoting speech language without sign language, touted to be the very best. There are two schools of thought on this; they exist to this day. The school of no signing believed in educating children on how to "hear" and function in a hearing world. The school of sign-based education believed in giving a child a language first.

At age seven, Dad was packed and enrolled. He was going to St. Louis which was several states away from home, away from all of his family. Dad only went home during holiday breaks. At the end of his first year, however, Grandmother yanked him out. She discovered that a child who used sign language at school was punished by being locked in a closet. Children were there to learn how to function in a hearing world. Sign language was not a skill promoted or allowed.

Dad finished his education closer to home at the Detroit Day School for the Deaf. He stopped going to school after the 8th grade. At first I thought this was perhaps because of his experience in St. Louis, but as it turned out, there just wasn't anywhere else to go. There were no high school programs for Deaf students in the Detroit area. The closest was Flint, Michigan, about two hours.

From stories I have strung together, Grandmother had no appreciation for the things Dad found joy in. She would cut his baseball games short and take him shopping with her. She took little part in his sports or other interests like fishing and bowling. She also had avoided his Deaf community of friends. When Dad turned 19, he made his way to Alaska. Once there, he asked someone to call Gladys to let her know where he was. I think this was a strong signal to his mother that she was no longer in control of his life.

Deaf schools educated students in a trade, so they could find a job once in the hearing world. In grade school Dad learned how to become a linotype setter. Dad traveled and lived in several major cities. To his advantage, he was a member of the newspaper union. He was able to find work in all the cities he wanted to explore. He ventured the West coast for a few years but ultimately returned to Detroit.

Grandma Gladys was the complete opposite of my Grandpa Sam. She was outspoken and blunt. Her eyes were always sad but her hugs were big and bold. However, she never shared stories of Dad growing up. She harbored underlying tones of anger and sadness. It was as if she was both at the same time, all the time. She would break down and cry at any given moment. She would cry during an argument, a holiday, or in the middle of a conversation.

Only now do I realize how much she had to cry about.

My mom Joan was born in 1942 in Covington, Kentucky to William and Lillian Montaster. She was born a hearing child. She, like Dad, was also an only child. At 18 months of age, she contracted spinal meningitis. One afternoon, Grandmother called out "Joan," but Mom did not answer. Again, my grandmother called out, this time a little louder, "Joan." Still no response. It was then at that moment that Grandmother knew there was a serious issue. They returned to the doctor and discovered that one of the side effects of spinal meningitis was the loss of her hearing.

In 1942, World War II was in full swing. Bing Crosby had recorded

"White Christmas" and "Silent Night," Walt Disney released "Bambi," and Anne Frank began writing her diary. In the Deaf world, the John Tracy Clinic in California was founded by the wife of actor Spencer Tracy and was named for their deaf son. The clinic provided parent-focused services for young deaf children. It was designed to inform hearing parents with information about raising deaf children. Neither of my parents benefitted from this information.

Mom grew up in a modest house in Covington, Kentucky, which was located across the river from Cincinnati. When Grandma Lillian researched how to raise a deaf child, she found St. Rita School for the Deaf, very close-by in Cincinnati. Starting at age 6, Mom went to school during the week, slept in the dorms and came home every weekend. The school taught ASL and had a program for speech therapy. Mom wore two hearing aids, which allowed her to be able to use the telephone. After high school, while living with her parents, Mom got a job at the post office, filing and sorting.

My memories of Grandma Lillian and Grandpa William are equally sweet. They were retired blue collar workers. Grandpa Bill, was retired from a factory job at Autolite in Cincinnati, a company that made electrical parts for cars. My grandmother Lill's last job was working at the retail store of Dolly Madison, a snack food store owned by Hostess. They were both proud of their work ethic and their daughter Joan. My Kentucky grandparents often shared stories of their childhood along with Mom's.

Between the ages of seven to 12, I visited Grandpa Bill and Grandma Lill for two weeks during the summer with Marty. For me, this provided a nice balance in the hearing world. My brother and I were completely hearing, so interactions between us and with our grandparents were totally vocal, not signed. I cannot recall a time where I thought Mom's parents felt raising her was a struggle. With them, I sensed a family support that didn't exist in my father's family.

The third question, *how did you learn to talk?* was always asked when people found out both my parents were Deaf. This question was the most logical. Nonetheless, it has been the most difficult to answer. Until I started writing this book, I did not have a clear answer. Reliving my life pushed me to examine much. At first, I had no idea how to answer this question. Every time I heard it, my brain started searching for an answer that might sound better than the last. My heart rate elevated from the anxiety of not knowing how to answer, *how did you learn to talk?*

Being a quiet, innocent, yet helpful girl, I wanted to correctly answer this obvious question. I felt obligated to answer. In my younger years, when teachers and adults asked, I responded with a shrug. Most adults probably considered this acceptable from an eight-year old. When I was in doubt, or when I did not want to talk about it, I just shrugged. But the more I was asked this question, the more it bothered me that I didn't know the answer. I also had no idea where to turn with my questions.

Research shows babies learn to verbally talk between 12 and 18 months with about ten simple words. However, by the age of one, I was signing approximately 50 signs. Other studies of sign language for infants point out that motor skills needed for speech develop between 12 and 18 months, but those needed for signing develop between six and 12 months. Babies are able to sign before speaking. It was interesting to learn that gestures made by Deaf parents can be viewed as singsong, the same as hearing parents do with their voices. Babies babble with both their hands and voices. However, with Deaf parents like mine, who used sign language there was an increase in the amount of "gesture babble" their infants used.

The more I was asked, *how did you learn to talk,* the more I began to scrutinize my responses. I started to speculate. How *did* I learn to talk? It never occurred to me to ask my parents. I figured they didn't know. I started to guess—the TV! That sounded good and logical! A box that made sounds, and I could hear the sounds. As I thought about my TV theory, I was afraid I'd be asked which programs I watched. I edited my answer to include Sesame Street for good measure. It was as educational as you could get in the '70s. When I threw in The Electric Company, another public television program aimed at counting numbers and making vowel sounds, I had the makings of a huge verbal vocabulary. I was more than pleased with this very rational answer. It had credibility. As I became more comfortable with my hypothesis, I further guessed that I also learned to talk from my hearing grandparents, crucial for my pronunciation.

In fact, when I was in the sixth grade, we were working on a science project in groups. As I talked about the wire connecting the battery to the light bulb, I pronounced it "whyer." Instantly, my fellow classmates ridiculed me. "Whyer, what's that?" I became embarrassed and contemplated why I sounded different than my classmates. I chalked it up to having hearing grandparents who lived in Kentucky.

My constant search for the "right" answers was an attempt to satisfy people's curiosity of my world. If they were asking, they were interested. Yet, why had I not been more interested to answer the question for myself? In fact, why did I not question the bicultural world I lived in as a child? I suppose it was because like any other child, I loved my parents. And to me, they were normal. And besides, my bicultural world was the only world I knew.

It wasn't until June of 2010 that I stumbled on the real answer.

Looking in the mirror, I asked myself, how did I learn to talk? I swayed my toothbrush back and forth like a symphony conductor. Who could possibly have taught me?

The back of my throat tightened.

"Come on! Think, Liysa!" I said out loud.

I cocked my head to the left, turned my eyes from the mirror to stare at the ceiling.

Again, I said, "How did you learn to talk?"

I set down my toothbrush, leaned forward on the bathroom counter, and hung my head over the sink. Suddenly something clicked. It was a fluid moment.

"My parents," I whispered.

My shoulders dropped.

"My parents," I said a bit louder.

Shaking my head side to side, I closed my eyes.

When I opened them, I stood taller, and looked in the mirror.

"Of course. My parents."

My parents taught me. They were not mute. Ok, I knew this all along, but never addressed it. You see, if you talk to Mom, you'll most likely understand what she is saying to you. She speaks quite clearly, though sometimes her L's sound like N's. Like my name. Liysa. She pronounces it "nisa." It's a nasally N followed by "esah." Dad, he has a deep voice like an out-of-tune bassoon. If you listen to him, you might struggle. I, however, can clearly hear what he is saying to me across the kitchen with my back turned. It's a booming baritone voice, and he pronounces my name Lee-cee. My parents have been talking to me my entire life, in two languages—a muffled oral one and a reinforcing sign language. From birth, both languages developed my cognitive brain and I received a double dose of vocabulary.

Why didn't I think my parents talked? I learned how to talk from THEM. Signing isn't talking. It is communicating. I never analyzed it. I suppose, since adults were in awe of how I learned to talk, I interpreted it as they were questioning ME. As if the *how* were a miracle. How could a child with Deaf parents talk? People associated me as a direct link to my parent's Deafness, to their lack of hearing.

During this time, I felt as though I didn't have a voice. I couldn't explain how I was able to talk, where I had learned it. Did they really think my Deaf parents couldn't teach me to talk? In reality, Mom and Dad's worlds were linked to my voice. I became their ears and voice in the hearing world.

SCHOOL

In the fall of 1977, I entered Kindergarten. I was excited to pick out my own clothes. Garanimals made matching clothes fun and easy. Interestingly, Garanimals was born the same year I was. The mix and match sets were designed with animals on the tags. My favorite outfit was my pants that were brown, yellow and green plaid painted on white fabric. I paired them with a green short-sleeved polo shirt. Both were pieces from the zebra line.

Every night before school, I took care in setting out my clothes, just as Mom did for work. She had routines and one of them was hanging up her clothes for the next day behind the door in the bathroom. In the morning, Mom watched the weather forecast on TV while she ate breakfast. This was followed by getting dressed. I tried to follow her routines. I did ok with setting out my clothes the night before, but not so great on getting out of bed in the morning. Dad woke me up by calling my name with his deep voice. The sound of his voice projected from the bottom of his diaphragm and he tried to be melodic like a bassoon, but it ended up garbled as the notes hit the air. This was orchestrated with his banging on my bedroom door. I became annoyed.

The first day of kindergarten Dad walked me to my classroom at Randolph Elementary School in Livonia, Michigan. When we got there, he signed good-bye and told me to have fun.

My teacher's name was Mrs. Hillstead, a tall, lanky woman with excellent posture. Her hair was nicely coiffed with curls curiously close to her head. They were tightly rolled but yet loose, enough for one to know her hair had been styled. She had pale skin and pale pink lipstick. Her cheeks were dusted with light pink blush. She looked like a porcelain doll with a warm smile. She wore a tan, below the knee skirt and a pale pink ruffled blouse. The woman was a palette for pale pink. Mrs. Hillstead was as nice to me as she was pink.

Kindergarten was easy and fun. I enjoyed it and was looking forward to the next grade. It set the standard for elementary. In first grade, my role was to share my native language. I was asked to teach the alphabet in sign several times during the school year as well as numbers and colors. It was always assumed I had a full grasp of the language. Teachers expected me to know the entire language even though I didn't know English fully. I was delighted to have more time in the front of the room. It was a glorified game of show-and-tell for me.

Years later, I learned that sign language actually helps with language and I.Q. A study conducted by Acredolo, L.P., & Goodwyn, S.W.* claims increased I.Q. has held up through age eight (the longest period studied so far). They revealed that in blind test groups, the children who learned physical gesturing and signs showed an increased I.Q. of between 8 and 13 points, compared to the equivalent groups who were not taught signing. This not only greatly increased early language skills but the I.Q. difference was still apparent when the same groups were tested years later.

Since sign language also helps with motor skills, it alleviates frustration in communicating. Nowadays there is a trend to use ASL to teach babies to communicate before they can speak.

As I entered second grade, I felt confident about sharing more about my Deaf culture. School became an excellent give-and-take setting that nurtured my need to teach people about the abilities of my Deaf parents.

At lunch, teachers handed over the class to lunch aides, sixth-grade volunteers who took us to lunch and recess. During recess, the lunch aides played with a few of us. They wanted to show off their new tricks of taking a magnifying glass and reflecting the sun to the leaves to spark a flame. While we waited for what seemed to be eons, I decided to show off my spelling skills. I said, "You know, if you take the G L off of glass, it spells ass." One of the sixth graders was appalled. She scolded

*(July 2000). The long-term impact of symbolic gesturing during infancy on IQ at age 8. Paper presented at the meetings of the International Society for Infant Studies, Brighton, UK.

me for saying such a thing. I thought I was pretty smart, especially since no one reported me. She went back to trying to create a fire with her magnifying glass.

In the third grade, my skill of reading people's body language was paying off and I used it to my advantage. During our December project in art class, we had a group project. On a cardboard cut out of a candy cane, we glued gazillions of 1-inch square red and white pieces of tissue paper onto the candy cane to fill in the stripes. Pencil erasers were our only tool. Over and over, small pieces of tissue paper were dabbed into glue and adhered to the candy cane cut out. When it came time to decide who would take the masterpiece home, Mrs. Kurtz, our teacher would sit down with the group. She asked for a number between 1 and 10. The student closest to the number would win the candy cane. As she began to write down the number, her other hand cupped her answer, so no one could peek. I watched the pencil move into a number 8. My eyes skimmed the group's eyes to see if they were doing the same thing. They were not. MaryJo was looking at the floor, Tony was staring at his pencil. No one else was thinking of this, no one else was watching her. She went around the circle. As each kid gave the incorrect answer, I became more excited. I was last.

When she came to me, I blurted out, "Eight!"

Mom hung the candy cane for years at Christmas.

In the fourth grade we had an egg decorating project. We were asked to bring a "blown out" egg to class to dress up for Easter. The night before, Mom helped me prick the ends of the egg with a pin and blow out the yolk and whites. The next morning was brisk and chilly. I had my egg in a plastic bag and met up with Molly White outside of the classroom doors before the bell rang.

Molly was my neighbor. She had blonde hair and blue eyes. She was taller than me by a few inches, enough for me to have to look up when talking to her. Technically we were friends. However, at the time, I wasn't sure what a true friendship meant. Since I didn't have many friends, I tolerated her mood swings even though they made me uncomfortable. She would switch from bossy to pleasant without any warning. I never knew which attitude I was going to encounter.

When I showed Molly my egg, she wasn't impressed.

"You're not very cool," she said.

My spine tensed up.

"Who decorates eggs? Babies do!"

My smile disappeared.

"By the look of your face, maybe you are a baby!"

I looked to the side and felt my neck turn red. I clutched the top of my plastic bag containing my fragile egg.

Molly took a step toward me.

Out of the corner of my eye, I saw her raise both of her hands.

"Hey baby! Listen to me!"

I flinched. As I did, she curled her hands into fists.

"If you want to be my friend, smash that egg." She took a swipe at me.

"Ok, Ok, just give me a second," I said as I tried to find a solution.

She dug her knuckles into her waist and said, "Ok, let's see you do it."

I thought of how hard Mom and I worked on that egg. I imagined her face when I'd have to tell her I broke it. At that, I reached into the plastic bag and took out the naked egg. I really didn't want to smash it. What I really wanted was to call her bluff, to challenge her to back off.

A fire began to burn in her eyes, she was getting impatient.

I thought to myself, stop being a wimp, what is wrong with me?

As I looked at her large forehead, I wanted to shout, leave me alone. Instead, I took one last look at the egg and with the crack of a whip I smashed it to the blacktop.

To this day, I don't remember telling Mom about what happened. I do remember how heartbroken I felt. As soon as the egg hit the ground and busted into a million tiny flecks, I wished I had never broken that egg.

My brother and I fought and bickered a lot. Sibling rivalry, I suppose. However, at night, our favorite time always started after we went to bed at 8:30 p.m. We had devised a few games that were played by yelling to each other through the wall. While we were both in our beds. My brother shouted, "Do you want to play a game?"

"OK, you go first."

"I'm thinking of an animal," Marty yelled.

"Is it big?" I replied just as loud.

He mumbled something but I couldn't hear him clearly, so I banged on the wall, then shouted, "Talk louder."

"Big? Yes, it's big."

"Does it have a long neck?"

"Nooooo."

"Does it a have tail?"

"Mmmm. Sort of," he grumbled. It sounded like he was yawning as he finished off with a mighty sigh.

"What do you mean sort of?" I asked. "Either it does or it doesn't?"

"Ok, then yes."

"What color is it?" We were supposed to ask yes or no questions, but I liked to break the rules.

Marty blurted out, "Grey."

"Ah ha," I said. "Elephant!"

I waited. "Elephant!" I repeated. Still nothing. I hated it when he played games while we were playing games.

"I saaaaiiiiid, an elephaaaaant!" I screamed. I arched my head to project my voice further. "Hey!"

By now anyone walking past our house would have heard me. Dad was at work but Mom was watching TV in the family room. In the evening, she took her hearing aids out, so I knew she couldn't hear us screaming our heads off.

"Maaarrrrtyyy!"

Silence.

I knew I was right and I wanted him to confirm it. I decided to get out of bed and check on him.

I threw the covers off and walked down the hall to his bedroom.

His bed was up against the wall, he was in it.

I walked to the side of his bed. I shoved my fingers into his shoulder to shake him.

His body absorbed the shove.

"Is it an elephant?!" I asked.

He didn't move.

I leaned my face over to look at him in the dark.

He was asleep.

I stopped for a moment, disappointed he didn't even last one round of the game.

I went back to bed.

Sixth grade became a right of passage. As the oldest class, we ruled the school. There were three classrooms with about 17 students per class. Molly and I were in the same class that year. As Molly and I continued our hot and cold friendship, I was still unable to voice my feelings. I didn't know how to speak up, not only to her but to anyone. She ordered me around. It was starting to bother me, but I didn't know what to do about it.

We were part of a group of five girls. Cindy, Debbie M., Debbie N., Molly and me. We were always together during recess. During outdoor recess, we knew our meeting spot was at a set of huge tractor tires of various sizes, cut in half, and planted into the ground. Our secret meetings were held in the largest of the tires. Our small bodies allowed for all of us to fit inside the cavity of the tractor tire. Sometimes we took off our jackets and hung them as curtains at the opening of the tire. We giggled and peeked outside. We treated it like our own little fort. We were a clique.

If we had indoor recess, we could either choose to play a game on the computer—Oregon Trail— on one side of the library, or we could browse through the books on the opposite side of the library. The girls and I mostly huddled in the book section where we tried to flirt with the boys. Flirting for eleven-year-olds was basically a form of teasing. Everything centered around "ha ha made you look," or "oooooh-aaah" comments.

The librarian, Ms. Kling kept an eye on us. She was petite woman and she had a black bowl haircut. Her eyes were wide and bulged from her face as if she was always on the alert. They seemed to bulge continuously when our group was in the library. We girls giggled and basically said nothing much. Ms. Kling constantly gleered at us, however, we never thought anything of it. We could never tell if she was relaxed or annoyed. Her eyes were always big.

One morning Ms. Kling took more notice than usual. Our group was becoming loud. We got into a noise-making contest to see who could be louder, the girls or the boys. We made silly sounds for no apparent reason. Ms. Kling had had enough and sent us back to class; we pranced and giggled, cracking jokes.

After lunch, all three classrooms gathered for another boring educational documentary. During the film, Mrs. Alden, one of the sixth grade teachers called me to her desk at the back of the room. She handed me a note and told me to go to the library and ask Ms. Kling for the film she had written down. I dutifully obeyed. I approached Ms. Kling, who was notably very crabby. I knew she was crabby because she sent us back to our room for goofing off. As she opened the note, I saw the question, since I was able to read upside down.

The slip of paper read, "Do you have Animal Kingdom?"

Ms. Kling looked at me and started to study me.

I grew a bit uncomfortable. So, I smiled.

Her eyes pierced through mine.

My eyebrows rose. I shifted my balance from side to side gently.

Ms. Kling picked up a pen.

I watched as she started to write. Her hand sternly printed the letters, Y E S.

She folded the small piece of paper and handed it back to me without making eye contact.

I paused, contemplating if I should even speak. "Excuse me."

Ms. Kling flinched in her chair.

"Um, I think Mrs. Alden would like to get this movie."

"No, she does not want the movie," she answered with a monotone voice. Her mouth moved widely as she enunciating each syllable.

My nose wrinkled. I thought, why would she send me to the library to get a movie?

Ms. Kling motioned with her eyes while she tossed her head back, to get back to class, however, I still believed that I was to return to class with a movie.

"Do you think it would be all right if you gave it to me just to be sure?" I lightly pleaded.

Ms. Kling now turned in a chair that did not swivel to face me eye to eye.

"No, Mrs. Alden doesn't want it, so please return to class now!"

I slowly turned on the back of my right heel and breathed out, "uh okeyyy."

I felt defeated in not getting what I came for, an Animal Kingdom movie. When I returned to the classroom, I handed the note back. I immediately tried to explain that Ms. Kling would not give me the movie. Mostly, I wanted to understand why. She opened up the folded slip of paper and thanked me. She told me, "It's ok, we'll get the movie another time." She then motioned for me to return to my seat.

A few minutes later, I noticed Cindy being sent out of the room. She was probably just getting a drink of water. When Cindy returned, Debbie was sent out of the room. I noticed a slip of paper in her hand. One by one, Mrs. Alden sent our group out of class during the movie. I kept thinking, does she need to know about more movies? I found it rather odd.

At the end of the day, Mrs. Alden asked me to follow her out into the hallway. I began to get nervous and hoped it was to explain why Ms. Kling didn't send the movie earlier. When I reached the hallway, the other girls and boys that were in the library with me that morning were also gathered. Mrs. Alden looked at each of us before she spoke.

"You all should be ashamed of yourselves," she said.

My eyes squinted together while I shook my head slightly side to side.

"All of you have behaved inappropriately."

I looked over to my left at the other kids. Was there someone else Mrs. Alden was talking to? I looked for any body language from my classmates that might help me decipher what she was talking about.

Mrs. Alden continued "You have been identified as making fun of the students from the Webster."

In my mind's eye, I pictured one of the students in a wheelchair. Once a year, our teachers coordinated field days with students from Webster. It was a special needs learning center. The kids there had braces on their legs and needed to wear them their entire lives. Others had bodies the size of a sixth grader, but their minds had not caught up. Some kids had short statures and limbs. The goal of joint field days was similar to a community service project and it was designed to educate us on these children's challenges.

"It is inexcusable to make fun of those children," she added.

My head jetted forward as my mind roared, what!?

"Ms. Kling observed all of you as mocking and imitating children from Webster."

My jaw almost dropped open, but I caught myself and felt the muscles in my cheeks spasm.

She continued the lecture, "These children are challenged daily."

My inner voice repeated, *challenged* daily.

"The struggles of being different are a great burden."

Again, my mind clung to, *struggles*.

Mrs. Alden explained, "It's not nice to tease these children."

My heart started to beat faster.

"You all have disappointed me greatly." She clicked her tongue, making a tsk-tsk sound.

My mind screeched ME? Is she really talking about ME? How could she think I was teasing anyone? I recounted the actions of the day.

Goofing around had led to Ms. Kling assuming we were making fun of the other kids. Ms. Kling didn't even know me. No one knew me.

I tried to figure out how this could have happened. How I could be associated to this kind of blame. Did the teacher and the librarian have a meeting in the teacher's lounge earlier? Did they come up with this scheme to try to catch us?

Mrs. Alden should have known me better. She knew about my background. There was no way she didn't know that my parents were Deaf? Hadn't she seen that I was challenged daily? Had I hidden my struggles or had she dismissed them?

My temper started to build. If only Ms. Kling and Mrs. Alden knew of how I was constantly teased. I started to rub my right heel on my left shoe as she continued to talk. I couldn't focus on her words because I was too busy reliving each insult I had endured in the past.

I thought my sixth grade teachers were aware of my parent's Deafness. It was something that followed me from teacher to teacher. It was something that was always brought up early in the school year. Everyone knew about my parents.

I began to chew on my lower lip as I heard only a few words in the teacher's lecture. I heard struggle. She was saying these children struggle. What about me? I struggled. I struggled to be positive and helpful while other kids mocked my parent's voices for the past five years. Kids exaggerated their voices and raised their hands next to their faces. Grunting and flicking their fingers, as if they were mimicking a monster. As a child seeing my parents being mocked, it broke me. I was so disappointed and cried often. Then, there were times when boys came up to me and flailed their hands in my face to mimic sign language and did it in a sarcastic way. It was more of a put-down. It was goofy and condescending.

Where was Ms. Kling to observe me then?

Teachers, recess moms, and school staff never witnessed it, or thought nothing of it. I never told anyone either. If I told, I was afraid of the attention it would bring; the teachers might have considered it trivial or the bullies would retaliate.

In each grade, I was asked to show the class my native language. However, it was as if teaching the alphabet was public reinforcement that I was different. It was another opportunity to remind the bullies of why they could make fun of me.

I began to realize how tired I was. I realized how heavy my heart felt. I had constantly been on the look out for opportunities to educate hearing people about my Deaf family. At the same, I tried to facilitate messages from the hearing world to my parents. Yet, I had just gone through my entire elementary education feeling invisible.

When Ms. Kling and Mrs. Alden brought me into this group and accused me of making fun of the other students, it confirmed to me, I had not been seen all this time.

As for any punishment from Mrs. Alden for "making fun" of the Webster students, there was only her you-have-disappointed-me speech. Little did she know that as I stood . . . I was already being punished: I was a sixth-grader who had just realized no one would understand my life.

I felt alone.

And so I shoved away the unjust accusation of making fun of the Webster students and turned my attention to the girls. I yearned to find someone who could relate to me. Obviously, no one could relate to being raised in a Deaf house, but I had to find some common ground.

I knew no one would be able to understand my bilingual, bicultural world. As far as I knew, my brother and I were the only hearing kids with Deaf parents in our city of 100,000.

Because Marty was born two years after me and adapted differently to having Deaf parents, I ended up being the family interpreter. It had as much to do with personality as birth order. At home, I continued to interpret phone calls and appointments. I was relied on to share information from my grandparents to Mom and Dad whenever they called. I compared my home life to other kids at school. I knew that I was responsible for tasks that they weren't even able to comprehend.

I was alone at school and I was alone at home.

Finding friends became very hard. As if everything happened at once, our group of girls was going through peer pressure. One afternoon, when Molly White was absent from school, our clique was convinced Molly was too pushy and for our own sake, we needed a DMAS, which was code for Dump Molly After School. Molly had problems. She liked to smoke, had boyfriends, and loved to be in control. She grew huffy when things didn't go her way. When the group decided to drop her, dumping Molly meant shunning her, not allowing her to sit by us at lunch and ignoring her. I secretly had felt like doing this for years. I just couldn't make that decision. Having the group do it for me was a relief.

When Molly returned to school, operation DMAS had been put into motion.

She wasn't allowed to be our friend anymore. No one talked to her. Molly caught up with me during lunch. As I turned from the hot lunch line to make my way to the table where the girls were seated, Molly ran up behind me.

"Hey," she said.

I stood in the middle of the multi-purpose room. I turned to look at her.

In her sweetest voice, she said, "Liysa, please be my friend."

I felt sadness come over me for what faced me, and her. It was the first time she had ever said *please* to me. Still holding a tray of food in front of me, I didn't answer.

A few seconds passed.

"You need to be my friend," she pleaded. Her eyes searched to connect to mine. Again, I was silent.

Molly stood a little straighter.

Slowly, I finally replied, "I'm sorry, I just can't." This was the excuse I had been waiting for to end our relationship. I couldn't stand it anymore.

"What?" Molly said, probably more surprised, than not hearing me.

I kept my composure.

Under her left eye, I saw a twitch followed by a flicker in her eyes. The same one I had seen with the egg episode.

I held my breath.

"Well, we'll see what happens, won't we," she said, her tone changed.

I tried to swallow. My throat felt empty.

She quickly turned and walked away.

Paralyzed, I still didn't move. After I had processed that we were no longer friends, I hoped I had done the right thing.

A few days later, Molly decided to retaliate. She enlisted the help of a few boys. It had been decided by Molly—she and I were going to fight. A fist fight.

Gossip spread throughout the sixth grade class and news of the fight reached me. All of the upper grades knew about it too. As the bell rang, dismissing us from school, my actions slowed. On this cold winter afternoon, I gathered my books, my coat, and hat. The back doors of the school flew open, and I felt the chill of the winter air freezing my blood. That caused me to move even slower. I was being released into unknown territory. I made my way out of the building and across the back field. In the middle of the field, a small thin layer of ice had formed. There was no other way to walk but across the ice. Kids were following me from behind and on either side of me. It was if they were herding me to the fight. As I walked across the ice, one of the boys was getting anxious.

He stepped in front of me, "Oohhh—you ready to fight!"

I managed to pass right by him. This got him even more excited, and he pushed me from behind. I fell to the ground, landing on my face and sliding on my chin. There was a cut. It didn't bleed much, probably due to the freezing temperatures. Molly was walking at the far right of the crowd. Afraid I'd be trampled, I scrambled to get up and regain my composure. As I walked down the final stretch of the school grounds pathway into the subdivision, the crowd of kids began to grow.

I reached the boundary that was considered outside of school property. There were even more kids. An enormous circle swarmed to engulf Molly and me. Within seconds, we stood face-to-face on the sidewalk.

Molly approached and stopped two feet in front of me.

She stared me down and said, "You're a bitch!" I skimmed the crowd of faces. None of the other girls that decided to dump Molly were around.

The crowd chanted, "Fight, fight."

I stood quietly, Molly nodded and yelled "Ok-go."

My body jerked forward as I realized I was being shoved. I landed directly into her hands. She grabbed my hair and slammed my head on the driveway of the home where the crowd had gathered. My eyes looked at the front door, desperately trying to will someone to come out of the house. I stayed kneeling on the ground, tears in my eyes. I couldn't stop bawling. My nose clogged up, and I wiped it with my mitten.

Molly yelled, "Come on. Get up."

I refused to get up.

"Poor little bitch," Molly said. To this day, I wonder if she kicked me or if a Charley horse suddenly seized my leg.

The crowd became bored and kids started to leave. I waited and eventually I was the only evidence left of the fight. At that moment, I realized what true loneliness was. I collected myself and walked home, planning what I was going to tell Dad. The cut on my chin had now started to bleed. The knot on my head throbbed. As I arrived home,

Dad looked at me and signed, "Happen. What?"

I explained that I was playing on the ice in the back field at school. I slipped and fell on my face. I told him I slid on my chin and bumped my head. It would do no good to tell the truth, what would a Deaf Dad do about it? He gave me an ice pack and a pat on my shoulder.

At school the next day, word had traveled to the teachers about the fight. I was called out from class. Molly was already in the hallway. As I made my way towards the other teachers and Molly, my stomach was in knots.

Molly's face was covered in band-aids. One plastered on her forehead. Others slapped on her cheeks.

I stopped in front of the three sixth-grade teachers and Molly. The single line they formed felt like a firing squad.

Mrs. Menley spoke first. "Liysa, Molly told us what happened yesterday."

I glanced at Molly and then back to Mrs. Menley.

"It's unfortunate that you two can't be friends," she continued.

I lowered my head and tried to fight back tears.

"After all, Molly was your friend and for you to start such a terrible fight."

My head shot up. I blinked as I tried to see who Mrs. Menley was talking to.

Mrs. Menley looked straight at me.

Me? Me?! They think I started the fight?

I took another look at Molly. A small smirk started to form in the corners of her mouth.

My mouth opened and I blurted out, "She's lying." But, I saw how pointless it was to continue. The teachers had already believed Molly. They didn't even allow me a chance to explain.

I didn't even get a hit in. Where was my witness? How come I didn't get a chance to tell my side of the story? I tried to analyze what just happened. How could she be hurt? Did she scratch her own face? Did the teachers even take a look to see if she was really bleeding under the band-aids?

One of the teachers turned to me and said, "I'm going to have to call your parents about this." She forgot, they could not hear. I nodded, again not bothering to explain. Inside I was grieving. I couldn't believe I had yet again been blamed for something I didn't do. I nervously waited for her to make an effort to contact my parents. Most likely it would be through me. She never addressed the situation.

I replayed that year in my mind several times after the fight. I became angry. I wasn't as angry with my peers as I was with my teachers. I felt as though I hadn't been noticed. No one admitted they saw what happened to me. The constant questions of living with Deaf parents came mostly from teachers and adults. Kids, meanwhile teased me about the way I spoke or taunted with flailing hands mimicking my first language. All the while my teachers accused me of making fun of other children and instigating fights.

I most likely had good reason to fight back, but I never did. I didn't know how to stand up for myself, especially against adults and teachers. I felt hopeless.

A few weeks before summer break, one of the girls in the clique decided to announce in front of me, DLAS. It was my turn to be dumped. After all I had been through with Molly and the teachers, I didn't even care that the girls decided to dump me after school.

Nothing phased me now, at this point I was so beaten up, I did not know how to care.

VACATIONS

Our 1979 Dodge Ram van was orange. A dark orange color that said, hippies. My parents bought it used. Mom and Dad were avid travelers via the great open road. They saved enough money for us to take a family trip every two years. There were two bucket seats on the inside front of the van and behind them a big open space. The floor and walls were lined with shag carpet. The shag was of course, orange, a darker orange and brown. There were two sets of double doors: one on the side to enter the van and the other at the back. My parents hired a carpenter friend who built a full sized bed in the back. Underneath the platform type bed was storage space. The double bed cushion was foam wrapped in fabric and was placed on top of the plywood frame. The ceiling of the van had a quilted texture and was a cream color. On each side of the double bed, were small windows with screens that when slid open, let in fresh air.

Mom sewed custom curtains for all the windows. The fabric was full of big bold orange flowers with brown and yellow elements. The curtains had to be shoved aside when we wanted to open or close them. Marty and I would open the curtains from the bottom, and then try to distract drivers by waving and making faces and then quickly shut them.

The orange van was now our luxury travel accommodations, complete with a small 3'x3' portable toilet set behind the driver's seat.

In 1981 my family planned the Walt Disney trip of a lifetime—Disney World itself in Florida. We left Detroit and headed south. Our first stop was to see Grandma and Grandpa in Kentucky. We stayed overnight. After that, the trip became very long. During the 80s, we weren't required to wear seat belts. So Marty and I would play in the back half of the van. We could be as loud as we wanted. We would roll from the bed to the floor or start to wrestle. When it shook the van, Dad would turn back and yell, "STOP!"

As we approached Florida, I was sleeping on the custom bed of foam. The heat blasted into the van when we rolled across the state line. I felt sweaty and blinked the beads out of my eyes. The sunshine along with the orange specked carpet was preventing me from seeing straight. We stopped at the visitor's center which was the gateway to citrus and Mickey Mouse. We pulled into the parking lot and I could smell oranges, not just one but an entire orchard full of oranges.

Our destinations included Daytona Beach, the Kennedy Space Center and then Disney World. At the Magic Kingdom's campground, they had movies under the stars and jamborees. On our first morning at the park, we rode all the big rides. My favorite was Space Mountain located in Tomorrow Land. After riding all the big rides once, we now returned to Main Street. This would be our educational piece from our vacation. We stopped at the Hall of Presidents, located in Liberty Square. I pleaded to go back to Space Mountain, and Mom struck a deal with me. After we learned about presidents, we could go back for another rollercoaster. DEAL! As we waited in line, Dad passed the time by sharing his knowledge.

Dad loved trivia. He could tell you every statistic for all the "hot" athletes. If Pete Rose was the "it" guy, Dad knew his batting average and his underwear size. Dad loved quizzing us on the state capitals, mostly because he had been to all of them, except Hawaii. Dad knew most of the presidents in order. Casual conversation turned into a home school lesson. "Who. First. President?" W-A-S-H-I-N-G....T-O-N, I finger-spelled slowly to be sure I got each letter. Correct. "Who. 16th. President?" I was excited, I knew this one. I spelt L-I-N-C-O-L-N in record time as I didn't even have to think about the placement of my hands for the letters. They just glided off my fingertips. "Who. 32nd. President?" WHAT?—I don't know. I instantly became defensive. I didn't know the home school lesson was for the entire time we were waiting in line. Dad asked me again. I twitched my head, I dunno. He told me it was Roosevelt and asked me to spell his last name. I wasn't really paying attention and I was sick of being grilled, so I refused to sign to him. I replied with a shrug which implied in sign language, "don't care." I shrugged over and over. Dad hated when I disobeyed, and he became upset with me. Mom chimed in with her own threat of not going on Space Mountain if I refused to sign.

I raised my right hand weakly and with my wrist very limp fingerspelled R-O-O-V-E-L-T.

"Come on!" Dad said.

I cocked my head to the side. "What?"

"Wrong. Try. Again."

I let out a heavy sigh.

"R-O-O-S-V-E-L-T" I then added, "Finish."

"No. Not. Right." He shook his head in addition to signing at me.

I stomped my foot and turned my body to the side.

"You. Know," he encouraged.

Mom added, "Go on, sign."

I glared back at her thinking, stay out of this.

Dad waited.

I waited.

Mom interjected a verbal, "Just do it."

No one budged.

Mom signed and spoke, "No roller coaster!"

"I. Want. Ride. Space Mountain."

"No." She shook her head back and forth.

I immediately turned back to her, "Why not!"

"You. Ignore. Dad."

"I'm. Tired. Not. Want. Sign."

Dad said nothing. He watched Mom and me.

"Then too bad, no ride," Mom voiced.

The line hadn't budged at all. It was the slowest moving line I had ever been in. I retreated to my thoughts. Why was I being given a history test?

We finally entered the show. I sat there, arms folded, refusing to tell my parents what was being said on the stage. Each time the audience laughed, I felt guilty. I knew my parent's didn't realize why the audience laughed around us. As the show continued, my mind formed the signs I'd use to interpret. My parents sat there, eyes faced forward. My heart flopped upside down, my fingers curled in and out nervously.

I couldn't handle them being left out. I turned and waved to Mom and Dad to get their attention. They both looked at me. I flippantly summarized in a few signs what was being said on stage. It was the best I could do since I was angry at them. I cared that they might feel left out. They both looked away. I huffed. They didn't even appreciate that I was thinking about them. There was no nod of gratitude or even a smile.

I got upset and sat there with my arms folded. I folded them to remind me NOT to sign. It was their loss that they wouldn't know what was happening.

When the show was over, we left the museum. My parents started to walk down Main Street. I lingered behind. When they turned in the direction in which I thought was Space Mountain, I quickly caught up to Mom and got her attention. I asked, "We. Go. Space Mountain?" Mom firmly said, "No!"

I was so hurt. My thoughts conjured up all the ways I had helped them. Even all the ways I wanted to help. I was nine and had Big Girl responsibilities, like making telephone calls for them and now, when I didn't sign the name of a president, I get denied a roller coaster. It wasn't fair. I was allowed to go on other rides, but it didn't really matter anymore. I wanted Space Mountain but that was non-negotiable with them.

Today, I understand this as their way of engaging in some conversation with their child. They wanted a teachable moment. When I didn't engage, it caused some tension in the communication. I also realized that my loyalty and love for them was so strong, I always wanted them to be included. It pained me to think they were left out, even if it was just a presidential show.

The orange van was still alive for another trip in 1983. Growing up in Detroit, I had already been to Windsor many times and a couple of times to Toronto. That year, we traveled to Halifax, Nova Scotia, then Prince Edward Island, and on to St. John's, Newfoundland.

In Halifax, we stayed with my parents' friends. Mom and Dad settled in by chatting and catching up on news. Later that night, the hosts showed us around town. We went Canadian bowling, called candlepin bowling. It was funny looking, but fun. I liked the bowling balls; they were smaller and cuter than the American version.

The following morning, our family was joined by their entire family, two parents and two hearing boys. I was eleven; they were 13 and 15.

We headed to downtown Halifax, a beautiful city on the harbor. Our first stop was the Halifax Citadel National Historic Site of Canada. I was in a great mood. Since we were traveling with older hearing boys, they were more than likely going to be asked to do the interpreting. After we paid admission, we waited just five minutes for the tour to begin. I was right, the older boy was asked to interpret. This was a big deal to me because I always had to interpret the tours, and I found them draining.

I dawdled in the corner of the exhibit, content with being able to hang out in the far corner and avoid boring lectures. Freedom: I made my way as far away as possible and found a comfortable boundary in order to avoid being called to come closer. As I turned, I noticed Mom with a line across her forehead. I darted my eyes over to the tour guide, who was in proper position—facing the crowd. I then jetted my eyes over to his left and yes, the boy was by his side. My first wave of anxiety disappeared; he was still there and so that meant he hadn't bailed. But as I looked closer, I noticed that while the tour guide was talking, the boy wasn't keeping up. As the tour guide finished about two sentences worth of information, the translation was only three words. Let me explain.

"On September 11, 1749, British troops completed work on the first Citadel. Unlike the current fort, it was built of wood, not stone," the tour guide said, then paused.

In sign language, my mother saw, "I-N 1749"

The tour guide continued, "As it turned out, it was the climate, not the French, which posed the greatest threat to this garrison. Fog, rain and cold winters contributed to its decay, as did neglect."

The tour guide paused again.

In sign language, my mother saw, "Bad. Weather."

The tour guide went on, "Meanwhile, Halifax continued to grow, becoming the capital of Nova Scotia when representative government was granted to the colony in 1758."

The tour guide paused yet again.

The boy signed, "Halifax. W-A-S Grow."

My mother was furious. She saw the tour guide was talking more than what the boy was translating. She was also becoming annoyed with the constant pausing.

Mom signed, "Wait. Wait." Both of her hands were extended in front of her, palms facing her and her fingers vigorously moving back and forth. But the boy never saw her.

A moment later, she spoke, "WAIT." The pitch of her voice carried louder than she knew in the building. The tour guide jumped.

I tensed.

"Nisa," Mom called as she scanned the room.

I let out a heavy sigh.

"Nisa," she said a bit louder.

My eyes connected with hers.

She waved me over. Her arm extended high, her hand cupped the air as she motioned me over. "Interpret, please."

My feet shuffled.

The tour guide watched me.

I did not say a word.

The boy had already resigned his post.

I took my position to the right of the narrator.

He looked down at me.

I looked up and nodded.

He resumed the lecture. "But a new threat was soon to appear. The outbreak of the American Revolution in 1776 again raised concerns that this vital British naval base would be attacked. The time had come to build a new Citadel."

My hands flowed parallel to his words. Mom relaxed and nodded. I signed, "New. Worry. Soon. Come. American..." Not knowing the sign or how to spell Revolution, I skipped letters and continued, "R-E-V-L-T-I-O-N. 1776. Again. Worry. England. Attack. Time. Build. New. Fort."

While I always wanted to please my parents, I didn't like the lectures. I didn't like history. I hated history. And the fact that I had to constantly translate it bothered me. Most of the time I didn't register the information because I was too busy listening to each word and matching it to a sign. For all those tours, museums, and attractions I had to interpret, I didn't take away anything from them. I was working. I now realize how mentally draining it was to interpret an entire tour. Since I didn't have a good handle on both languages, my brain worked hard to compensate my limited knowledge of complex historical signs as well as decipher what the tour guide was talking about.

Our vacation also took us to Quebec.

While in Quebec, a predominately French speaking region, major tourist signs were written in French and English. On our route we stopped at a roadside hot dog stand. Without being asked, I exited the van with Dad to help him order. The stand was on a clearing just off the road. We took a few steps uphill. The service window was a hole cut out of the side of the wall. As we approached the small shack, there was a man waiting to take our order. He leaned onto the small wooden counter on his right forearm.

"Bonjour!" he said.

I answered for my father, "Hi."

He continued in French.

I looked to Dad and shook my head side to side.

Dad looked confused. He glanced at the gentleman and then back at me.

"Tell 'em we like hot dogs."

I turned to the man who was staring at my father.

"We would like to order some hot dogs."

He heard me talking and turned his head quickly to me.

I smiled.

The vendor stood up and continued talking in French.

I looked at Dad. I pointed to my mouth and then signed, "I don't know what he's saying," which was more of just a shrug than signing the entire sentence.

Dad again took a look at both of us.

I looked puzzled.

After a few moments my father gestured to the French man. He put his fingers to his mouth and then raised four fingers. He then found a picture of a hot dog on the menu that was laying on the counter. The gentleman reciprocated. He rubbed his own belly, and gave him a thumbs-up sign. Dad completed the order with fries and sodas. As we waited, the man talked to Dad. I was in awe that the man didn't speak English but was communicating well with Dad. I didn't even have to help get the conversation back on track.

There have been several times I've had to interject a sign or translate an idea to get my parents interactions with their hearing acquaintances back on track. Many people assume that Deaf people can read lips. It's another question I would have to answer often. Technically, even professional lip-readers can only capture 30% of what's being said. The idea that all Deaf people can lip-read is strongly held. But many conversations are somewhat anticipated. If my parents were at a school function with me, my teacher was most likely going to discuss what happened in an educational environment, so words like homework, play, grades and writing are already anticipated. When a hearing person found out they were talking to someone Deaf, they immediately talked louder. When they did that, their facial expressions shifted and the enunciation of the words looked different. The placement of the words drawn out could be hard to read. Men with mustaches can be tricky to figure out. Their facial hair covering a good portion of their lips is distracting. Also, if someone had an accent or their English was broken, the likelihood of the words being visible diminished. Lastly, hearing people don't face each other when they talk. There are statistics that report men do not face each other, but just as many females don't either. Once, when a retail cashier helped Mom at the check-out and discovered she was Deaf, it never occurred to her to speak to her eye-to-eye.

Our last major stop on our Canadian journey was Ottawa. We had a private tour scheduled at the Parliament. My great uncle David A. Croll was a Senator. He wasn't able to be there when we arrived but approved our back stage tour that most civilians don't get to see.

During our time in his office, the concierge gave us a long winded history lesson that I happily translated. I adored my Uncle David. I didn't know him very well, but he was very kind to my parents. When I did see him, he always smiled, took my hand in his, and gently cupped it with the other. His smile filled me with the same warmth I felt when Grandpa Sam smiled.

The last of the great family vacations was in 1985; we went to California. We didn't have the orange van anymore. In fact we didn't have a very reliable car, so Dad borrowed my grandmother's ugly green sedan. It had a big back seat and that's where Marty and I hung out or slept. We cruised the Western Plain, stopping at Wall Drug, Mt. Rushmore, Black Hills, a prairie dog farm, Las Vegas, San Francisco and all the way to Tijuana. One of the stops was Los Angeles; the World Games for the Deaf was being held here.

The World Games for the Deaf was like the Olympics for those with a hearing loss. It was a two-week event. My parents decided to go to the track events. They were held at the UCLA campus. I found the arrangement as just one more Deaf outing which was like the picnics I attended regularly. During the games, the athletes performed high jumps, hurdles, pole vaulting and shot put. But I didn't see any of it. The events took place down on the track, but my parents were socializing on the platform. I couldn't wander off too far. We attended just one day of events.

The following day, a group of Deaf people decided to meet at Universal Studios. When we arrived, the group formed at the tram assigned for our tour. An interpreter was scheduled. I was pleased. This had been the first time I ever heard of scheduling an interpreter for an attraction. I became giddy and excited knowing that I would be able to fully enjoy this tour.

I was confident this was going to be an awesome day, because arrangements for an interpreter was a guarantee I didn't have to do it. As I started to daydream and wait patiently for our tour to begin, I was oblivious to the time that had passed. I sensed something out of the corner of my eye. The group had huddled. I tried not to pay attention. But my curiosity wanted to know what was going on. A deep baritone voice called out, "Lee-cee. Lee-cee"—I turned to see my father motioning me to come on. Finally, the tour was going to start.

As I got closer, Dad said, "Interpreter. Not. Here," and added "You. Can. Sign. For. Us?" A no-show, just my luck. I nodded, signing, "Sure."

Everyone loaded into the tram. I boarded last and was instructed to stand between the tour guide and the tram driver at the front. I was 13, and felt like I was on stage. The attentive audience was facing me as I held my balance. The tram rolled forward going through the front lot of Universal Studios. The pavement was smooth and I felt comfortable at my station. We saw offices and sets from television shows. When the tour moved onto the back lot, the trail was no longer paved, and the tram rocked as it hit the uneven trail. This was where the more elaborate movie sets were staged. They were still intact. We passed the Bates Motel from Psycho and another set from Jaws. The information was not too technical and turned out to be an easy gig. The tour came to an end. Pleased that I wasn't feeling exhausted, I exited right after the tour guide. I had to wait for my parents because they were seated in the back.

The tour guide turned to me. "You are an honorary employee," she said.

As people departed the tram, they thanked me. It was very genuine.
One man exited and reached out his hand.
I extended mine to give him a handshake.
He shoved a dollar bill in my hand.

My eyes bugged out. "Thank you," I signed.

He nodded his gratitude.

I skipped in place.

Another woman exited and smiled at me. "Thaaak uuu," she voiced.

I nodded to her and signed, "Welcome."

She reached into her purse and gave me a five-dollar bill.

Yeah! I thought.

One by one people gave me money. I thanked each one. I was unable to contain my skipping and bouncing.

I had no idea interpreters got paid. I just never thought about it. All in all, I earned thirty bucks. I calculated that to be over a dollar a minute. I then realized, I had done some extensive interpreting in the past—someone owes me some money!

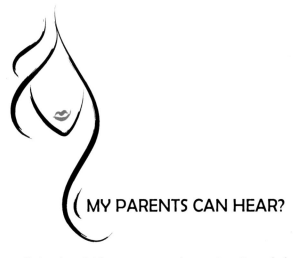

MY PARENTS CAN HEAR?

Being inquisitive even as early as nine, I tended to question more and more of my surroundings. My imagination blossomed. Since my parents were the only ones in the neighborhood who were Deaf, my imagination started to wonder why my parents *pretended* to be Deaf. I speculated that they were either spies or they were taking notes of all my bad behaviors.

Since my interests were not heavily into espionage, I decided my parents were not spies. However, I still thought they could hear me. I envisioned a huge notebook filled with notes about when I translated the wrong words for them. I wasn't swearing yet, so the book was a reminder for me not to swear. I didn't want them jotting down another thing about me.

They must be able to hear, I convinced myself. There were times when Marty and I would be in the living room wrestling. We'd jump from coffee table to couch. Our coffee table was as long as our couch. We used it as a giant slide. Leaping from the couch landing on the table and gliding the length of it until it dumped us on the floor. Our energy ramped up each time we took a turn. My father was two rooms away in the family room. Within a few minutes, Dad stomped his way toward us, yelling for us to stop. We quickly stood still in our places. Marty and I looked at each other, laughed, and as he went out the doorway, we bolted back to the couch to slide. Within a few more minutes, Dad became furious. We were sent to our rooms.

How could he have heard us? It didn't make sense.

There were many times when Mom and Dad answered our questions when we weren't even looking at them. Once, when I was in the kitchen, I went to the refrigerator, looking for butter to set out on the table. I stood with the refrigerator door open unable to locate it. I bobbed up and down skimming each shelf. I mumbled to myself, where is it?

Within a moment, Mom spoke in her unique pitch, without signing, "Look on door shelf, right there." How did she know what I said?

Mom told me to make our beds often. Without signing, I talked under my breath, "Why?"

Mom answered, "Because I said so."

Marty and I continued to test their hearing many times. We took turns whispering around Mom and Dad. Not necessarily behind their backs, because that would be too easy. It was spontaneous.

So one day when my parents were chatting in our family room, I turned to my brother. "Say something," I said in the spoken word.

My brother looked at me, searching for a word. Then he said, verbally, "Boo."

Nothing happened. I signed to him "again" just in case our parents were listening.

My brother said, louder, "Boo!" adding an extra ew sound at the end.

Our parents didn't respond. Now I wanted to know the truth and told Marty to scream it. He looked at me without even questioning the repercussions and let out a huge, "BOOOO!"

Mom jumped slightly in her seat. This is it, I thought. She's going to reveal that she can hear us. She touched her ear, and it looked like she was adjusting her hearing aid. I knew she could hear us. But when I looked closer, I saw that she wasn't even wearing it. My brother, meanwhile, had turned himself back to the TV, no longer interested in testing our parents.

I, on the other hand, was not going to give up investigating our parents' abilities to hear. I devised a new plan.

One afternoon we were on our way to visit Dad's family, Grandma Gladys. Marty and I were in the backseat. Mom was wearing her hearing aids that day. Good. I was ready to test her again.

I gently leaned a few inches forward. "Mom," I whispered.

Nothing.

I tapped her shoulder. "Turn up radio," I signed and pointed at the car radio, followed by a swift twist of my hand. This was to motion turning up the volume knob.

She did. I plotted my next move.

"Mom," I said in a flat voice.

Nothing.

Determined, I yelled with more conviction and repeated her name. "MOM!" "MOM!"

She moved her head to the side.

I could tell she was trying to avoid my screams.

I continued again and again, "MOM," "MOM," "MOM," and "MOM!"

She finally caved in and whipped her head around and said, "WHAT?"

Startled, I replied, "Um…nothing." Then like any kid pushing the limits, I quickly added, "No one said anything."

She looked at me. With her nasally accent she said, "I can feel your voice on my neck."

This concluded my quest. They were Deaf all right, but only in their ears. They had other ways of hearing.

I began to learn how vibration played a significant role for someone Deaf. Other senses heightened to compensate the loss of hearing. What did the pounding of the floor feel like to my father two rooms away? I imagined the floor was a super big highway of electrical cords. The moment we jumped, the electricity bolted through the floorboards in the direction of my father. My father's feet then absorbed the tingling shake of the floor under him. As we repeated our jumps one after another the bolts shot out on my father's nerves. Zap. Zap. He'd have to find the source.

The vibration of the floor as my brother and I jumped all over the living room alerted my father two rooms away that we were goofing around. Likewise, the vibration of sound traveled from my mouth and landed on the back of my mother's neck. I'm not sure if my parents ever knew that I doubted their deafness that year. In comparison to the hearing families I knew, it just seemed too unique to be true.

Years later, after I learned about Dad's sensitivities to vibration, he complained about how loud the car radio was while we were driving. The music pulsed under his feet, and he asked me to turn down the music. I moved the volume dial down barely with my finger and thumb. A few moments later he complained again. I cupped the entire knob with all of my fingers, turned my hand to lower the volume; however, I never grasped the knob. The music stayed at the same level. Depending on how badly my father was agitated by the music, he would either notice or live through it.

D.A.D. CLUB

When I was finally convinced that my parents were Deaf, I too wanted to be Deaf. I wanted to be just like them. I imagined going to Deaf Club just like them. I was proud to have them as my parents. They were good people. They had values and worked hard. They were dedicated to their jobs.

Mom worked the day shift, Dad, the night. They had worked out a system for raising a family, earning a living, and contributing to their Deaf community.

Mom was an employee at the Northville Recorder, a small local newspaper, transcribing script into a computer. She worked there more than twelve years.

Dad worked over twenty years at the Detroit Free Press. He was a linotype printer and laid out words for printing. The words were called "slugs" which were made from cast metal. The slugs were individual words. My father was to lay out the frame and insert the words from his bin of thousands.

Dad was a member of the D.A.D. (Detroit Association for the Deaf). It was a formal club with by-laws, voting members, and elections. There were several Deaf Clubs across the country in the more metropolitan communities. When my father traveled, he could find a club and network with people in that city simply by finding the Deaf club.

Members of the D.A.D. club were very fortunate to have a place of their own, a single story building with a basement in downtown

Detroit. The main entrance was through a double set of glass doors. The vestibule opened into a hallway and to the right was the coatroom. The coatroom was a gathering place for all the kids where they played hide-and-seek during the winter months. A hundred coats were lined up, and children hid between them. The chase was the best. We screamed and plowed through coats to try to scramble out of the room first.

At the foyer, a door off the hallway opened into the bar. Several hightop chairs and tables were arranged. There was seating all along the long bar. It was a big room with a jukebox. The jukebox cranked out tunes. The volume was automatically adjusted to blaring. Every time someone put a quarter in, the songs belted out so loud on the tiny jukebox speakers that they were almost unrecognizable.

On the other end of the building was a multipurpose room. It was huge, like my school gymnasium. It even had a stage at the far end of the room. Here the meetings were held along with DINGO games. DINGO is Deaf bingo. Letters weren't called out. Instead, there was a digital board that illuminated the letters for players.

The D.A.D. club also hosted several family friendly events. Bambi was one of the first movies I saw on movie night. It was closed captioned.

At home, we had a closed captioning decoder box called the Telecaption device sold by Sears. In 1980, Mom ordered one for $250 from the catalog. After Mom was notified it had been delivered to our local store, we went to pick it up. It was the size of an old stereo receiver. Our unit had two knobs on the front. One was to control the TV channel, when there was only local programming. The other knob was used to control the text to "on" or "off." When we returned home with the unit, Mom hooked it up to the back of the TV. When Mom tuned in Happy Days, the text on the bottom of the screen appeared. It was like Christmas morning; a squeal of delight filled our family room. Mom clapped and beamed.

Another barrier was now removed.

Up until this time, Mom and Dad had to guess what was being said on the TV. Dad watched sports, so the need for captioning to him wasn't critical, but Mom loved movies. She loved the black-and-white movies. Now, she could go back and watch them again and understand the plot.

Shows like Laverne and Shirley, Love Boat and Three's Company were captioned. But, the news was not. Even as a seven-year-old, I found it perplexing that the important news was not captioned. I was called upon from time to time to help inform them of select news stories. It would be another year until Mom and Dad could have a wide selection of viewing options with captions. Not all shows were captioned, but they were satisfied with what they had.

This was ten years before the Americans with Disabilities Act (ADA) law was passed in 1990. The Television Decoder Circuitry Act required all televisions larger than 13 inches sold in the United States after July 1993 to have a special built-in decoder that enabled viewers to watch closed-captioned programs. In 1996, the Telecommunications Act required the Federal Communications Commission (FCC) to adopt rules requiring closed captioning of most television programming.

At Christmas that year, the D.A.D. club put on an awesome event. The hall was jam-packed with kids. Deaf kids and hearing kids were all over the place. Santa and his elves always visited. The elves called children up to the stage by age groups. When they called up my age group, I excitedly but cautiously walked up to Santa. I wore my favorite blue corduroy jumper on top of a white blouse. I wore cream tights and black shoes.

As I approached Santa, he looked similar to the one I envisioned to be at the North Pole: big tummy, white beard, and a very red suit. I stopped five feet in front of him.

Santa signed, "Hello. Little. Girl."

I raised my hand to say hello.

"You. Good. Girl?"

I tried to concentrate on both his hands and his lips but I could not see his lips through his white beard.

"Yes!" my fist nodded up and down.

"Good."

I smiled.

He motioned for me to step closer.

I kept thinking, I didn't know Santa was Deaf!

Santa waved his hand again, "Come."

I moved forward slowly, again, wondering why Santa was Deaf.

Santa's arms reached out for me.

I climbed into his lap.

"What would you like for Christmas"? Santa signed.

I deduced this from the signs that looked familiar, "Want. Christmas."

Santa placed his index finger to his chin and then to his chest. "Tell me," he said.

I straightened up and signed the first thing I could think of, "A bike!"

He gave me an "A-OK" gesture and winked his right eye.

I guessed that he was going to check his list to be sure I was a good girl and deliver it to me on Christmas morning. An elf (I recognized her as one of Mom's friends) appeared at Santa's side with an unwrapped gift. Santa helped me down off his lap, and I was given the board game, Operation. As I walked off the stage hugging my new toy, I was still confused. Was Santa Deaf?

Dad waited at one side of the stage near the stairs. As I walked to meet him, my thoughts were on Santa. It was magical, because Santa signed and asked me what I wanted. I always found the mental imagery of sign language powerful, and when Santa signed, "Tell me," I wanted to tell him so much more.

The previous year, the Santa at the mall had verbally asked, "What do you want for Christmas?" But, now seeing that same question signed had more of an impact on me. I felt as though I could have shared all my feelings, thoughts, and wants with him.

I hadn't felt this way before. My exchanges with Dad were rarely emotion or feeling based. It was always very matter-of-fact.

As I made my way down the stairs from the stage, Dad smiled. His tall frame crouched down to inquire about what Santa had given me. I tried to sign "game" using both hands, but the bulky box was slipping, so I mouthed it to him. On my final step off the stage, I took my position next to Dad. I thought about all that I wanted to share with him, my questions, fears, and all the times I was teased. I longed for Dad to say to me, "Tell me."

Instead, my role was to "Tell 'em." And so, I took my position next to my father, where I stood devotedly for many years to come.

Deaf Club was a place my parents could go to communicate and socialize freely. It was a great outlet for them and for me. Marty and I could play for hours. I wasn't interrupted to translate or facilitate a conversation when I was at Deaf Club. The only time my parents called me over was to introduce me to one of their friends, the way that parents do to show off their kids.

My family traveled countless miles to connect and be with others.

They did so to escape the isolation they felt in a hearing world. Our Deaf organization had sports teams and competed in leagues and in tournaments with other Deaf clubs in the Midwest. I remembered the excitement of going to tournaments and picnics that brought hundreds of people. It was a full day of events. Here, I was a kid. We arrived in the morning and left at bedtime.

At Deaf Club, everyone was able to communicate barrier free. At these events, we were one.

When I got older, I didn't go to Deaf gatherings as often. Partly because I could now stay home alone and partly because my parents wanted to be without kids. I was also becoming involved with my hearing friends. As a teen, I still went to a few Deaf events well after my brother had abandoned going. I wanted to hang on. I enjoyed chatting with Mom and Dad's friends. I enjoyed sharing news about my life. I could fully explain my thoughts and concepts. It was freeing. But, once I got my drivers license, I stopped going. I felt I didn't belong at Deaf club anymore. An internal feeling told me I was now hearing and needed to be with my own kind, in the hearing world.

Deaf clubs are practically non-existent today. The D.A.D. Club building in Detroit was sold. The group now rents space for their gatherings and meetings. My father continues to be a member, now for over 50 years. Due to technology and the effort of recruiting younger members, Deaf Club has changed to be more of Deaf meet-ups, gatherings and conferences.

The Detroit Association for the Deaf Club that I grew up with is gone.

Hearing

HI NEIGHBOR

On a summer afternoon, the phone rang just as Mom and I were going shopping. I was excited to shop for back to school clothes, after all I was entering the sixth grade. I turned to Mom and signed "phone" to let her know I was going to answer it. She knew it was ringing because in our house, when the phone rang, the kitchen lamp and family room lamp flashed.

I reached for the phone. I said, "Hello."

"Hi, dear, how are you?" a woman responded.

I was not sure whom I was talking to, but responded in the monotone, "I'm fine."

"Is your mother there?" the caller asked.

I replied with my standard answer for telemarketers. "No, my mother is Deaf." I quickly added, "She can't hear you."

"Oh, that's right, I'm so sorry I forgot," she laughed.

I tried to figure out who was on the phone. Someone who already knew Mom was Deaf.

As if reading my mind the caller said, "This is your neighbor, two doors down."

My mind mentally counted the houses, knowing there was only one neighbor to the right, and then several houses to the left. I said, "Oh, Mrs. Johnson? How are you?"

I knew Mrs. Johnson because she was on my newspaper route.

"I'm fine. Listen. I wanted to tell you about a new modeling class at the center, would you like to hear about it?"

My heart pounded with excitement. "Yes, please!"

Mom looked over to me and motioned, "Come on." I raised my index finger and told her to wait a minute. I then cupped the phone between my ear and my shoulder and signed, "Woman. Two. House. Down." I pointed in the direction of her home. I didn't sign Mrs. Johnson because I was pretty sure Mom didn't know her name.

Anxious to get the information about modeling class, I turned back to Mrs. Johnson on the phone.

She went on. "Well, I need to ask you a few questions first, would that be ok?"

My head nodded and before she could even finish, I said, "OK! Sure!"

"What's your eye color?"

"Brown." I envisioned myself in high fashion clothing.

"What's your hair color?"

"Hmm, my Mom says it's a dirty yellow color." I saw myself glammed up in hair and makeup.

"You mean blonde?" She chuckled.

My face flushed. In sign language, blonde is signed by using the sign for yellow—pinky and thumb in a "hang loose" hand shape, the thumb at the temple, then flicked backwards as if tossing back your hair.

Mrs. Johnson continued, "Excellent great, and I know how tall you are, so I'll just jot that down."

In my mind, I had now walked into the Barbizon modeling agency. I saw the runway where I'd practice my catwalk. I was delighted to know Mrs. Johnson thought of me for the class. I couldn't wait! Modeling would help me be prettier and fit in.

She went on. "I have just another couple of questions."

I paced the floor excitedly.

"So, dear, when you are sleeping at night, do you ever find your hand down below?"

I stopped walking. My breath felt like it had been knocked out of me. I spoke just above a whisper, "Down below, what?"

She chuckled again, "It's ok, dear."

I froze.

She continued, "When you wake up in the morning, do you find your hand on your private area?"

I blurted out, "No," forcing the word into the phone.

"Ah ok," she replied.

I frowned. How did this relate to modeling?

Mrs. Johnson continued with a soothing tone, "Let me ask this another way. . ."

There was a pause. "Have you ever rubbed your vagina?"

The blood drained from my body. I was speechless. My feet felt like lead.

Meanwhile, Mom had grown impatient and stomped her foot on the floor to get my attention. The vibration on the floor pumped the blood back to my heart and brain. I turned to look at Mom in slow motion.

"C'mon on," she signed.

I nodded my head, which meant, "Ok, finishing up."

"Um. . . Mrs. Johnson. . . I gotta go, my Mom's calling me."

"Sure honey, no problem."

"Thanks!"

She added at the last moment, "If you want to come down and talk to me more about the class, just stop by. You can invite a friend too."

"Thank you, Mrs. Johnson, I will."

I hung up, relieved the phone call had ended, and yet strangely elated that she still considered me for the class. Her last line of questioning was startling, but her voice was soothing. I hadn't reached puberty yet, even though my friends had. I was still flat-chested. The timing of her questions was when I felt awkward about my body. However, since she was an adult, I thought I was supposed to allow her to ask me what she wanted. It was the first time I felt that level of discomfort. It was the first time an adult made me feel dirty.

I purposely wiped away any confused looks from my face. I wanted to forget the personal questions Mrs. Johnson had asked. I was embarrassed and didn't want Mom to know what had happened. I felt disturbed. I don't think I could have even signed those kinds of things to my mother. I didn't even know the sign for vagina. If she knew what was asked of me, I was sure she wouldn't let me go modeling.

As I turned to walk towards Mom, she asked, "What. Talk. Phone."

I told her the truth—about a new modeling class.

We went shopping. When we returned home, I got permission to find out more from Mrs. Johnson. Even though I was uncomfortable, the possibility of modeling was appealing. I was impressed she though of me and I felt obligated to find out more about the classes. Because she said I could bring a friend, I called Tammy. I didn't want to be alone should there be more questions. Fortunately, Tammy agreed to come with me.

As I took a step onto her front stoop, I pictured walking the Barbizon runway again. I knocked on the door and Mrs. Johnson answered. However, she only pulled open the big wooden door, requiring me to talk through the screen door.

"Hi!" I cheered.

"Hi Liysa." She looked puzzled. "What can I do for you?"

"Um, I'm here to talk about the modeling class," my voice cracked. She peered at me," What modeling class?"

"Uhhh, uhhh . . . ," I said.

She tilted her head a bit. I interpreted that as, I'm waiting.

I said, "The one you called me about on the phone."

She shook her head side to side "I didn't call you on the phone."

My face grew hot. I began to feel like I was in a twilight episode.

She took a step back from the door.

Tears started to form in my eyes.

Mrs. Johnson looked at me, nodded and said, "Ok then."

I realized the conversation was about to end.

"Ok, bye." Mrs. Johnson said as she pulled the door in front of her.

I suddenly remembered Tammy, standing next to me. I wanted to rush home and avoid any questioning. Tammy, meanwhile, sneered and poked me in the ribs. I turned and looked at her directly, scared. Then I said, "Bye" and leapt from the door stoop as the door shut behind us.

I was already three strides in front of Tammy. Before she said anything, I stammered, "I must have been confused, maybe it was a different Mrs. Johnson." Then I told her I had to go home.

I ran through our back gate and into the back door to my house. Mom was watching TV. I threw up my hand for a fast wave to show her I had returned.

Looking back, I now realized how much resentment had swept over me. I had been betrayed and unprotected by my own mother. I had had to deal with this on my own. Why couldn't my Mom hear? If she could have, I wouldn't have answered the phone in the first place. Besides, a hearing mom would have picked up by my tone of voice that something was wrong. If she could hear. . . but she could not.

I went directly to my room, plopped onto my bed, and cried. I felt humiliated, naïve, and stupid. I spent the next hour trying to re-count how this could have happened to me. Exhaustion took over. The next morning I pushed the whole episode to the back of my brain. I never spoke about modeling classes again.

Mom never asked about my conversation with Mrs. Johnson or modeling class. At the time, I was relieved I wouldn't have to relive the horrible experience again to her. I was afraid she would have thought it was my fault and that I should have known better—because I was hearing.

The next summer while I was visiting my maternal grandparents for our traditional two-week vacation in Kentucky, Grandma Lill offered to enroll me in a fashion class. It was a class that taught young girls how to apply make-up, the "in" hair styles, and trending fashion tips. I adamantly declined. My mind filled with memories from the Mrs. Johnson call. I didn't want to go, at all. My grandmother was confused; thinking this would be something I would enjoy. I continued to decline without an explanation. I was still scarred from the humiliation I felt and I associated it to any fashion, make-up or modeling class.

Ten years later, I reviewed the episode. After suppressing this memory for a long time, something jogged it free. When I tried to replay the conversation, I hadn't really figured out how I got Mrs. Johnson confused with the caller. Now, wiser, I realized I had been pranked. The obscene caller had never said her name. I had provided her with one and she went with it, a true manipulator.

Now, as an adult my thoughts turned to how I could have been so naïve? Living in a bicultural, bilingual family, I probably wanted to be accepted more so than my hearing friends from hearing families. With my desire to fit into the hearing world, I grasped at any opportunity, including modeling class.

But then, when I reflected on this more, I realized, it wasn't about being accepted by the hearing world. It was stereotypical adolescent angst. I had low self-esteem because of my unique world, but I was like any other girl. I wanted to fit in. Body image, fashion and the pressures to be popular probably were more of a concern than finding my place within the hearing community.

NO SLAM DUNK

Frost Junior High was made up of seventh and eighth grades. For me, it was a new beginning; one that I hoped did not include my having to educate people about my Deaf parents. I hated the questions, and more than the questions, I despised the hand flapping. Kids would come up to me flailing their hands in my face as they mocked, "What am I saying?" They were mostly joking but still interested enough to see if they accidentally signed something. I cringed at the sight of flailing arms, wanting to yell out, "You just called yourself an asshole." But I didn't. Instead I absorbed the flailing arms and the insults, because I longed to blend in. If I blended in, then no one would take notice of my background.

I thought I'd fit in better if I did not mention my parent's deafness, ever. However, within a few weeks, word had traveled. The bullies from elementary school found another way to ridicule me. They knew I was an easy target, so they urged some of their new friends to carry out more teasing. I could be counted on for tears and to any bully, tears were the ultimate sign of victory. Now, more people knew about my parent's deafness than I wanted. I felt as if the entire school was talking about it.

Meanwhile, my brother Marty seemed to sail through elementary school without any taunting, at least none I knew about. I used to think that he fit in because I paved the way for him by getting the bulk of the teasing. Then I used to think it was because he was a boy and perhaps not as sensitive as I was. Now looking back, he probably never acknowledged my parent's deafness in a way that enabled others to exploit him.

The harassment took a different turn. It wasn't even Deaf-related anymore. Once, when I was in the cafeteria, I exited the hot lunch line carrying a tray of hot food with my favorite item, chicken patty on a bun. A boy, whom I had never seen before, raced up to me. He looked me straight in the eyes and with one flick of his wrist, knocked the tray of food from my hand. It flipped and landed on the floor. As he ran off, I felt like every set of eyes in the lunchroom was on me. I knelt down to pick up the mess, and when I passed a garbage can to my assigned lunch table, I threw out my entire lunch. I then took a seat on the bench by the wall towards the end of the table. I sat there, hands at my side, head hung low and cried. The tears streamed fast. I tried to hold them back, but they rolled fast down my cheeks, like a waterfall. I managed to slow the tears down. As I wiped the tears with the back of my hand, I now saw clearer. I looked down towards the opposite end of the table. Three boys were pointing at me and still laughing. They snickered "chicken patty, chicken patty." I wanted to disappear.

The bell rang, lunch was over. I stayed seated. Students around me rushed to get to their next class. I failed to move. My feet were attached to the gym floor as if glued there. As time passed, I took notice of my surroundings. The janitor folded the benches and tables back into the wall. Lunch ladies cleaned up the milk station and hot lunch line. I got up thinking, "Why does this happen to me all the time?" I just wanted to be left alone! I wanted to go home sick. But I knew I would have to explain why, both to the office and Dad. I walked to the office, stopped at the door, put my hand on the doorknob but at the last second, I decided against it. I went to my next class.

Bullying not only scarred me then, but for many years to come. Nearly twenty years later, whenever I saw chicken patty on a menu, I cringed. When I cringed, my brain flashed a mental image and I could see myself again, as I stood in the middle of the cafeteria. I felt a quick fast jab in my gut, reminding me of something I wished I'd forget.

Eighth graders at Frost Middle School were encouraged to select an extra curricular activity they'd like to join in high school. Sports and clubs were looking to recruit new students. The process was very blasé. Sign up was in an empty classroom, which was also the after-school detention room. During selections for Churchill High School, each department or sport posted sign-up sheets. Some were eye-catching. The really decked out sign up forms with red and black streamers and balloons, the schools colors, were from the cheer and pom-pon squad. However, most were just a single sheet of ruled paper slapped up with scotch tape. I entered the room alone. Alone again—I wasn't really planning on signing up for anything. I browsed the options, not really moved by any of them.

Up until then, the only extra curricular activity I had been in was one year of YMCA T-ball and two years of dance in elementary school. One year was tap, the next jazz. During my tap year, I was in the fourth grade. Our dance teachers were choreographing the finale to God Bless America. The instructor knew my parents were Deaf and asked if I'd like to sign the song for them. As soon as the teacher said, "for them," my immediate need to please my parents kicked in and I said, "Yes." I went home to practice the signs to the words. I had no idea what the sign was for "God" and "bless." When I asked mom, I was surprised she knew them. My parents didn't go to church and I had never seen those signs before.

As the recital approached, I worked hard on my performance. I would be standing in front. I loved the spotlight. A few hours at home before the rehearsal, I was getting visibly nervous.

Mom asked, "What's wrong,"

I said, "I don't want to mess up."

She smiled and signed, "Don't worry. No one there will know sign language, and you will be fine."

She was right. When it came time for the finale, I took my place and belted out a visual God Bless America. I found my parents in the audience, middle section, 42 rows back. The whole time I was signing, I kept thinking, I hope they can see me.

Dancing had stopped because money was tight. However, Marty still played hockey. Our parents loved the games and we went all over the state of Michigan for his tournaments. I didn't understand how they found the money for hockey and I couldn't continue with dance. My interest turned to hockey since Mom and Dad still allowed Marty to play. I figured I could too. I enjoyed watching it, which probably meant I'd also enjoy playing it.

During dinner one night, I waved at Mom to get her attention.

She looked up from her meal.

I signed, "I would like to play hockey."

She looked puzzled, and then voiced, "NO!"

"Why not?"

She replied quickly, "It is for boys. Not girls."

"Please," I said, "let me try."

I then remembered there was a girl in elementary who played hockey on a team. There weren't any girls teams in our city, so she played with the boys. If she could, why couldn't I?

"Mom!" I jammed my thumb into my chin harder than I would have liked. "Why not?"

I saw her brush off my request as her fork jabbed into a potato.

Dad was at the stove behind us and had not seen our conversation. When he sat down, I tried to ask him.

"Dad," I signed with a wave to get his attention.

He looked at me.

"Can I play hockey like Marty?"

Mom jumped in, "I. Finish. Said. NO!"

My brother was quiet. The look on his face told me, I'm not getting involved. I'm not sure if Dad agreed with Mom or just didn't want to start any more trouble. He hung his head low, sucked on his teeth to make a tsk sound and hummed, "Noooo."

Generally, Dad would yell and then I yell back which resulted in an argument. This time, the way he shook his head at my request made me realize it was going to be pointless to even try to continue this battle. My mind rushed to so many things I could have pointed out, like how did we have money for hockey but not for dance. But, I never dared to talk about money. Dad returned to his meal again. I felt deflated. Without dance, I had nothing to do.

A few years ago, I mentioned to Mom the situation in which I explained I wanted to play hockey. I reminded her that she told me it was for boys. She laughed and said, "I did not." I spent a few more minutes trying to help her recall the conversation. She still didn't remember. I didn't know what to think.

There were so many sign-up sheets. Many I had never even considered or knew about before. I wasn't musically inclined, so I passed the sheets for band and choir. Even though the pom-pon and cheerleading squad had great sign up sheets, I didn't think I'd like it. As I read and passed more forms, there were the obvious no's. Football, no. Soccer, no. Tennis, no. Swimming, no. Drama. I stopped. I stared at the white lined ruled paper that was plainly labeled DRAMA in the top margin. A few kids were already on the list. I told myself I had no previous experience to be considered for drama. I imagined an intense interview that required me to quote Shakespeare, followed by a quiz on the era of Romeo and Juliet. The drama teachers would discover I had never been on stage, rejecting me from the limelight. At the same time, I determined drama would be hard for my parents to understand. I would be speaking and not using sign language in the plays. How would they know what I was saying?

The previous year, my parents took me to see Helen of Troy. It was done entirely in American Sign Language with Deaf actors. It was boring. I didn't understand the plot. There were no voice interpreters to translate the play. I couldn't really follow the signing on stage because my attention was wavering due to the overwhelming noise in the audience. It's amazing how loud Deaf people can be, they are not quiet. They can't hear the noises they are creating, so to me it always seemed extremely louder.

As I tried to watch the play, my mind kept going to the shoes shuffling a few rows behind me. I heard people breathing around me. A few rows over, there was a couple talking, not paying attention to the play and the smack of their hands grew intense. Their conversation escalated to an argument.

And to top it off, Dad fell asleep.

I decided not to sign up for drama. I didn't want Dad falling asleep if I was Helen of Troy. I forced the desire for acting out of my brain.

Still, I felt a longing to be apart of a group. As I came to another sign-up sheet, it said GIRLS BASKETBALL. Anxiety set in. I had gone through all of the sign-up sheets and this was the last one. I contemplated basketball the same way I did drama. I had no experience. The only time I picked up a basketball was in gym class. I didn't even know if I was coordinated.

Other students seemed so sure of their interests. I imagined them signing up for their respective activities with confidence, which kept me thinking, how did they know what they wanted to do? Most of them were already involved in their respective interests which may have been an easy choice for them. I found it grueling. I recalled the numerous basketball games I had attended with my family. It was during a time when Dad played for D.A.D. Club league. I deduced basketball would be something my parents could support. I wouldn't have to explain it. Dad knew the game and it was visual, no interpreting would be needed. I signed up. Turned out, I didn't account for the fact Dad worked nights and my games were after school.

Looking back, it had never occurred to me to seek my parent's opinion to join drama. Actually, my parents and I never had in-depth discussions. We never talked about things I liked or my plans for the future. While we communicated decently, it was mostly stories or news of our current activities. Mom and Dad's stories were long. A simple grocery trip was described with each and every move, aisle by aisle. As they searched for the Jiffy peanut butter and then moved throughout the entire store, each item described as they crossed it off their list one by one. The re-enactment at the register was so detailed I could see the cash being exchanged.

When it came to discussing my academics or activities, there were short interactions.

"How. School?" Dad asked.

"Fine," I said

"Homework?"

"No."

When I told Dad I joined basketball, he said, "Good." He then shared a few pointers on how to shoot the ball. No one ever asked me, "Do you like it?"

During high school, I secretly wanted to be in a school play, yet I never even tried out for one. It wasn't rejection I feared; it was how the rejection would fuel the bullies. I didn't want to be teased for failing. One afternoon on my way to the gym for basketball practice, I passed the auditorium. A rehearsal for the upcoming school play was in progress. I stopped in the middle of the wide hallway and looked through the open theater doors. The stage lights were on; the actors were at their marks, and the director was seated in the middle section of the third row. Jill's blonde hair glistened in the lights. She recited her lines to her partner. He was shorter than Jill and also had blonde hair. He may have been a senior. I watched intently. I took a deep breath and exhaled so hard, my body felt every regret I had. I should have tried out for a play. My heart was heavy. I longed to be on that stage! I thought again as I had so many times before; if I were in a play, my parents would not be able to enjoy it.

A bell rang. I jerked myself out of my daydreaming and walked to the gym for basketball practice.

Mom and Dad came to a handful of games during my three years of basketball.

And then, my senior year, I quit.

When it came to the outside world of my Deaf home, I felt like I had to figure it all out on my own. I felt that way for a very long time. I had hoped each new job, activity, or hobby would prompt Mom and Dad to see my talents. I hoped it would excite them. If they were excited, then I knew I had picked the right thing.

I carried this characteristic with me for many years later.

Was I happy? Sure, on a day by day basis. However, it wasn't until I was 35 years old, that I discovered something called joy. I finally embraced the ideas, hobbies, activities and lifestyle I had always wanted. I was stuck trying to make other people happy with my decisions. With each new interest, I looked for approval from someone, friends, family or even teachers. But, when I didn't get it, I abandoned my newest interest. Approval can be a hard thing to accomplish, the harder I tried, the harder it was to accomplish.

As a teenager, I felt like I had been constantly helping Mom and Dad survive, while no one taught me how to live.

I wished I had asked Mom and Dad more. I wished I had gone to them with more questions, more ideas and more feedback. However, since I was always in a role of knowing—I thought I knew it all.

HIGHER LEARNING

I got my first "real" job when I was fifteen. My friend Kim had just gotten a job at Cloverdale Ice Cream in Plymouth, and I wanted to work with her. They were hiring. When I asked my parents if they would let me work there, Dad said, "No." I don't even remember why, but I pleaded for a couple of days. Mom helped me convince Dad, and finally, I was given permission.

When I got my driver's license, I took a job at Silvermans, a men's clothing store in Wonderland Mall. It was more money because I made commission. On my very first day, I sold an entire suit along with extra shirts and ties for options to the first customer I approached. I had fun and the job was a fit to my personality. I enjoyed matching people with what they were looking for. After eight months, the general manager was looking to fill a manager position at the Novi Mall. They asked if I was interested. I was elated they thought of me. When I asked Mom and Dad for permission, my father objected.

"Why?" I asked.

"Too. Far." He said.

"The Novi Mall is another ten minutes," I said. Again, I pleaded with him for days.

He refused. I didn't take the job. Looking back, I wished I had asserted myself, but I wasn't wired that way. I had been molded to be helpful to my parents, not to cause them grief.

I had six different jobs by the time I graduated high school. I quit my last job so I could have my summer off while I prepared to go away to college. I was enrolled at Ferris State University in Big Rapids, Michigan. A month or so before fall semester, I was filled with anxiety. This was going to be a big move for me. I started to regret my decision, mostly because I'd be away from my parents. They had relied on me for so many things. I wasn't sure if Marty would be around to help out. He didn't seem interested and was always with his friends. I felt guilty to leave them. I notified Ferris State that I would not be attending. I planned to attend Schoolcraft Community College. I didn't even ask my parents. I just thought it was best. When I told them, they said, "Whatever you wish."

What I needed, was for them to set me free. I needed for them to tell me, "We'll be here when you need us." Or, I needed for them to say, "We'll be fine." For them, they probably didn't realize how I felt. For me, the insecurity of leaving them wasn't only a young girl out in the real world; it was years of being a young girl with an even bigger role.

One afternoon I was sitting on the back patio with my parents. Casual conversation somehow got twisted.

"Why. You. Late. Last night?" Dad said.

"I dunno."

"Tell me."

"Just went out," I replied.

"Don't like." He added, "You. Must. Follow. My. Orders."

Orders? I thought. I just graduated high school. I was sure that meant I was able to live freely.

He wasn't concerned about my future college plans. He was only concerned about his control on me, and my curfew.

"Leave me alone," I scoffed.

I got up to go inside.

"Hey," Dad yelled.

"What?" I yelled back without signing. My heart rate immediately shot up.

Dad's face frowned. "Listen. To. Me."

I turned my back on him and started to enter the house.

"Come. Back," My dad called behind me.

With one foot in the house, I whipped around to face him and screamed, "NO!"

I grabbed my car keys and left for a few hours.

Dad and I already had disagreements about what I should do with my life, as was the case with the management job at Novi Mall.

Finally, I rebelled. Molded or not, I had to fight for what I wanted. Except I didn't know what I wanted. I only knew that I was tired of arguing with him. So I ran. I ran away as far as I could go, Ferris State. I reenrolled. I had to get away from the Deafness, the co-dependency and the arguing. I also thought when I left, they would be sorry. They would need me soon enough.

Thus began my journey into the hearing world, full-time.

While at Ferris, I happened to stumble on a job posted at the local high school. It was for a sign language interpreter position. My curiosity got the best of me, so I applied. When the principal interviewed me, he asked me to show him my skills. I had to translate a paragraph from a history book. The principle didn't know sign language and I waited for someone to come into the room, but no one did. He said I could start at anytime. After translating the paragraph, he offered me the job. I thought, this was going to be a piece of cake, so I took the job. This was before sign language interpreters were required to be certified.

I was assigned to a sophomore. Her name was Marie. She had some hearing, wore two hearing aids and knew sign language. I didn't meet her until my first day on the job. As I took my seat at the front of the room for history class, I sat up straight and put on my best performance. The young girl seemed to nod and understand. Easy! The next hour in study hall, I had a chance to talk to Marie.

She was a tall girl, wore glasses and was thirsty for communication. She quizzed me on how I knew sign language as she peeked from the corner of her eye to the boys at the next table. I didn't know if she was trying to see if they were gawking or she was doing the gawking. I learned that she had been main-streamed for her schooling; she had always been the only Deaf girl in her classes. She was on the cheerleading squad and she was boy crazy. In less than thirty minutes, I was exposed to a new generation of being Deaf. I also sensed that her parents pushed her to be engulfed in the hearing world. I wanted to tell her all the great things about the Deaf community. I wanted to find young Deaf kids for her to network with and share with her the benefits of being with peers. However, I did not. Marie wanted to be friends and asked if she could call me through the relay operator from time to time. I told her it was ok.

I continued signing for three of her classes. The classes became harder; I noticed my inability to keep up. This was not a piece of cake. What I didn't anticipate, however, was the distraction I was to the other students. I tried to be professional but boys from her classes were shoving notes in my hand in the hall. Some of them were only a year younger than me. Apparently, the last interpreter was 54 years old. So putting an 18-year-old, signing, in the front of the class was a distraction. And, I too was boy crazy.

I realized several things: I was a distraction to the class, Marie craved a friendship with me, and interpreting was not easy.

After six weeks, I quit, never feeling like a quitter, but only thinking of what to do next.

I transferred from Ferris after my first year and enrolled at Michigan State University, mostly because my boyfriend at the time was there. The large classes were different for me. I shared my economics class with 200 students. I sat in the back row and people-watched.

As a sophomore, I was placed in an all freshman dorm on the outskirts of campus. Walking to classes took over thirty minutes. I didn't feel like I fit into the dorm life, but in order to move off campus I had to be a part time student. So I dropped down to part time. I made up the difference in credits at Lansing Community College. Again, with no direction and only thinking I had myself to guide me, I changed majors several times. I took astronomy, fashion, and foods.

I finally settled on paralegal, since Grandma Gladys hoped I'd be a lawyer. She was also paying for my education. It was the least I could do to please her. I discovered a paralegal program at Madonna University located in Livonia, one mile away from my parents' house. I moved back home. I was right back where I had started.

My final year at college I took on a heavy load, mostly because I had lost credits bouncing around from school to school. I took 15 credits my fall semester, 18 in the winter semester and 21 in the spring. In addition to my current waitressing job, I was job shadowing for six of the 21 credits. I made the Dean's list that last semester.

During my final semester in 1994, my maternal Grandpa Bill died. Mom and Grandpa were very close. Mom often commented that her carpentry and painting skills came from her dad. After the funeral, there was a shift in my house. Before this time, I don't think my mother ever experienced depression. I had never seen her sad. I saw her angry, but not sad. I, myself, knew depression, I knew what it was like to get really down and become irritated, removed, and irrational.

One weekday morning, Mom was cleaning the house. I was sleeping in. It was close to 11 o'clock and she was aggravated. She wanted me out of bed. She asked me to help her with a phone call, even though she could use the relay service that began in 1991 by the state, the Michigan Relay Service, It was to help provide equal access to Deaf people. When a Deaf caller wanted to call a business or hearing person, they called the Relay first. They placed the phone on the TTY and then dialed an 800 number to reach an operator. The operators answered the call on their TTY. While on the line, they called the phone number the Deaf caller wanted to connect with. They acted as the go-between for the call, typing the hearing caller's words and speaking the Deaf callers typed messages. Most calls averaged fifteen minutes or more, never less.

As Mom banged on my door, I ignored her. I knew she could make a call if she really wanted. My mother became enraged, so I got up. I made the phone call that took three minutes. Annoyed that she had gotten me out of bed I yelled and signed at her, "There. Happy!"

She yelled back, "Not. Nice!"

I smirked, said nothing.

"I. Not. Like. Your. Acting." Mom said, then added, "Out!" as she pointed her finger towards the ceiling.

Out?

My brain scrambled to translate *out*.

Was she really kicking me out? My temper soared.

Move out, fine!

I packed a bag and went to Missy's house, a close friend. A couple of hours later, Dad came to find me. He asked me to move back. I was so angry I couldn't think straight. I declined. My father wasn't yelling, he just asked. I only saw him as trying to control me. I wasn't thinking about anyone except myself. I refused to talk to either Mom or Dad. I was grateful for Missy's family. They allowed me to stay at their house until the end of my school year. It was a month away. I know I caused extra stress for them.

As graduation approached, I decided to invite my parents. I went home to visit them. When I entered the house, there were no hugs, just waves and hellos. We sat at the kitchen table. I was again at the top of the pyramid.

"Graduation. Two weeks." I signed.

Mom and Dad nodded.

"Can. You. Come?" Raising my eyebrows which indicated I was asking.

Mom and Dad nodded again.

"It will be held in Southfield," I explained.

"O.K." Dad said.

Not knowing what to say next, I went on and gave them the location, date and time. I handed them the tickets to the graduation ceremony. l wasn't sure if they would really show up. Their nods seemed to just appease me.

As I sat on the main floor of the gymnasium with the other students of the graduating class, I searched the bleachers. Missy was going to be there. I knew if I could find her, then I'd know that my parents made it. I moved my eyes and I caught a glimpse of someone waving. It was Missy. Seated next to her were my parents.

I felt a sense of relief. I was glad our stubbornness had not become regret.

DIAMOND IN THE ROUGH

In February of 1995, I moved to Chicago. Mom didn't say much about the move, though my father objected. We argued but it didn't last long. He saw I needed to explore. My first job as a paralegal was in worker's compensation, which I left after six months to work at Ford Motor Company in dealership litigation. It was a contract position, and I could be let go at the end of my contract.

I had just met a boy from Chicago a month before on New Year's Eve—that was enough to get my bags packed. He found me a lead for a job downtown as a paralegal. I applied and got the job. I dumped the boyfriend a month later.

I lived in an apartment in the Lakeview area of Chicago, one block west of Lakeshore Drive. My morning commute was a 15-minute express bus ride on the CTA (Chicago Transit Authority) to the Stone Container building in the Loop. It's the iconic building in the skyline where the top depicts a diamond.

I felt free in an amazing city to explore where no one knew me. I was tired of being responsible, so I started to live irresponsibly and focused on instant gratification. I partied, a lot. I didn't save a dime and I lived day to day. The days revolved around ME. The nights revolved around ME. The weekends were all about ME.

But after about six months of partying, I felt a void. I started thinking about going back to school. I wasn't satisfied at my paralegal job. After logging more billable hours in eight months than my coworkers had in a year, I was passed over for a bonus. My boss had no idea how much I worked because she was out three days a week. I began to disengage from the work.

I didn't have a TTY when I lived in Chicago. One Sunday morning, I had slept in, hung over from the previous night. The phone rang.

"Hello this is Michigan Relay Operator 563234, a hearing impaired person is trying to call you, have you received a relay call before."

"Yes, this is Liysa GA," I said, knowing that the Go-Ahead was going to be followed by a long pause. Relay operator calls were time-consuming.

I heard a click.

"Hello?" I checked.

Mom said, "Hi Liysa, how are you?"

I choked up.

"Oh, GA...I mean say GA," I heard her add.

I was shocked.

"Um, hi Mom. . .GA."

"I'm call you use V. C. O." Her voice was clear as if she was right next to me.

VCO stood for Voice Carry Over. I had heard of it but never used it. The relay operator would still work in the same fashion by typing my words onto her TTY screen, but now Mom could read the words and respond verbally using the three-way calling option.

My mind kept saying, mom is on the phone. My mom is calling me on the phone. I figured the more I mentally repeated it, the more I could believe what I was hearing. I had heard her voice before on the phone made to our grandparents in Kentucky. While in high school Mom did use the phone with her hearing aids, but she stopped after I was born. Mom dialed Grandma and Grandpa's phone number at an agreed upon time. Grandma and I trained Mom how to use the phone to ensure we would hear her voice. We taught her that after she dialed the phone number, she should count to ten. This allowed me or Grandma to get to the phone in time. After counting to ten, Mom would shout, "Hello Liysa. Hello Marty." There would be a small pause as she caught her breath and she continued with, "Mommy and Daddy love you. Bye."

During these calls, Marty and I never had the opportunity to respond. There wasn't any back-and-forth dialogue. However, now with the VCO, the relay operator didn't have to translate the broken English of her typed words. The interaction was faster than the traditional relay call.

"This is amazing," I said, as my voice trembled and I stifled a soft cry.

There was a long pause.

Suddenly, I realized I had forgotten to say GA and the operator chimed in, "Is that a Go Ahead?"

"Oh, umm, yes. . .GA." I stammered.

The relay operators were trained to type everything they heard. Mom responded with, "Why are you crying?" I tried to explain my emotion, what a simple phone call could do to lift a spirit.

I answered, "I'm Shocked, GA."

The conversation lasted only a few more minutes until Mom said, "OK. Good. I just wanted to try VCO. GA."

I thanked Mom for calling as tears dripped from my chin.

It had never occurred to either of us to use VCO again. To this day, I don't know why. When a friend called this *heimweh*, which is German for homesickness, I thought, ridiculous. Why would I be homesick for hyper-responsibility? I was free, free! Another friend conjectured doppelganger.

"Doppel what?" I asked.

"Double walker," she replied.

I frowned.

"I could be way off," she said, then added, "Your shadow self, your spirit double."

The word *double* hit me. I had been in two worlds, this I knew. And yet, I had somehow denied both of them. So, where to start?

Dad was still bowling in tournaments all over the Midwest. During the first year I lived in Chicago, there was a tournament in Milwaukee, so I drove there to surprise him. The amazing thing about entering a bowling alley filled exclusively with hundreds of Deaf people was the noise level. It was eerily quiet. Practically the only sound was that of the bowling balls being dropped on the lanes and the subsequent crash they made when they slid into the pins. There was the clear voice of a waitress several lanes away who called out, "I need two burgers and fries." The walkways in front of the alleys were filled with bowlers and spectators, chatting. I stood at the registration table and wondered which direction I'd find Dad. I knew enough to just be patient. My ears were on high alert. A few minutes passed, and then, there it was—a big booming belly laugh that blared out like an exaggerated chuckle. "Ahhhuhuuh ahhhuhuuh." It sounded like the giant from Jack and the Beanstalk. It was the sound of Dad's laugh that rose above all else. I made my way past the shoe counter and heard the low chatter of the staff. I walked further and picked up unclear grunts to match the smacks of hands in the air deep in conversation. I overheard many conversations with my eyes. The couple to the side discussed their teammate's high score, and a mother told her son "no more money," most likely for the video games or food. Two feet in front of me, a man stood on the balls of his feet with his arms extended in the air. He signed to someone behind me, "Miller Lite."

I walked toward the sound of my father's laugh. He looked up and seemed shocked to see me. I said hello and gave him a hug. Settling into the unfamiliar surroundings, I noticed familiar faces. I felt comforted to know so many people. A sense of home took over. What I wasn't expecting was the kind of attention I was getting from a few bowlers. Men started to flirt with me. My interactions were significantly different than when I was a child. Back then, I was asked, "How old are *you?*" It was a way for me to demonstrate my signing skills when I was introduced to my parents' friends. The question, however, changed as I was asked, "How old are you, *now?*" to inquire if I was legal.

Dad quickly shared with me his own observation that I was being hit on. But I brushed it off. Besides, the guys were old, like forty. I wasn't even interested.

I noticed Dad's demeanor was different and I couldn't understand why. I didn't realize at the time, but I think I was infringing on his life. I was being exposed to a different Deaf experience, Dad's world. In the Deaf world, you grow up in community. I assumed Dad didn't want me to know about his past. I think he feared I would be told exaggerated stories reminiscent of a younger time. Stories that weren't appropriate for your children to know, nothing bad, just adult.

I wondered did Dad want to keep his Deaf world separate from me, a private world, where he could be himself? Up until this point, I only knew what he wanted me to know. Now it was clear: I had grown from being his child to an adult. During that visit to the bowling alley, a boundary line had been crossed, one that I wasn't aware of. Yet.

Back in Chicago, I searched the want ads. I found an interpreting agency in the northern suburbs of Chicago. I was intrigued. I knew I had lost some of my signing abilities, but I wanted to check it out. I had only learned about professional interpreting a few years before. In my senior year at Madonna, I needed an elective. I enrolled in the Deaf Culture class where I learned there were professional interpreters. At that point I didn't consider switching majors for I was graduating in a few weeks. It had never occurred to me to even consider being an interpreter. Besides, I had already changed majors several times. The goal was to graduate.

I made an appointment with the executive director who agreed to assess my signing skills. I took the train to Mt. Prospect and luckily the agency was only two blocks from the station. As I walked into the office, a large round man greeted me. He had a grey beard, dark eyes and a warm smile. He reminded me of those big teddy bear type guys. I had an impulse to hug him. He shook my hand and introduced himself as Dr. Clearing. He didn't look like a doctor. He motioned for me to take a seat in the chair across from his desk. As he walked around the desk, I noticed his Doctorate on the wall.

"So, thanks for coming Liysa. It's nice to meet you."

I sat up straight, my eyes focused on his mouth. "Thank you. Same here."

"Before we begin, if you don't mind, I'd like for you to take the assessment tests first and afterwards we can chat."

"Sure, yes…sounds good."

"We are going to have you interpret a video to test your signing, and then we'll have you voice a video to test your receptive skills?"

I winced as I took in the word "receptive." I had never heard of it when used in reference to sign language. My palms began to sweat.

"Is that ok?"

I realized I hadn't responded. "Oh, yeah, yeah, let's do that."

I interpreted the practice video to a young woman in a different room. I put my best hands forward and demonstrated my sign language skills. I visualized how I would have signed it to my parents. I even visualized my parents in the room as I diligently informed them of the information on this test video. It made me more assertive in my quest to look qualified. The woman jotted down some notes after I completed the video. As I began the next session, it dawned on me that receptive skills meant, the "reading" of sign language. I had never connected reading sign language to be a receptive skill. I felt more confident, and again a test video appeared. I strung together my best English to illustrate my skills. Again, in my mind, I placed my parents in the room with me. The lady thanked me and led me back to the director's office.

"Tell me a little about why you'd like to become an interpreter."

I scurried to find a reason. "Um, well, my parents are Deaf and I've been doing it for them," I said weakly.

"I see. Your parents are Deaf, so you are a CODA"

My head tilted to the side. I squinted. "A what?"

"CODA, Children of Deaf Adults."

I nodded. I kept thinking, I'm an acronym?

"You haven't heard of it?"

"No." I shook my head.

He reached into the massive Rolodex on his desk full of index cards. Post-it notes stuck out of several of them.

"Let me give you this lady's name. She's a CODA and an interpreter."

I began to get impatient and waited for him to find the number. I had no idea why we were talking about this. He wrote down the number and passed it to me.

I shoved it in my purse without even looking at it.

"Ok, so let's talk about your signing, shall we."

"Let's."

"After taking a look at your skills, as a CODA. . ."

My inner voice groaned, uh, there's that word again.

He continued, "I consider you to be a diamond in the rough."

I nodded. Now we were getting somewhere, I thought.

"You just need to polish up a little on your signing," he continued.

My mouth became dry. I pressed my lips together and moved them to one side.

"If you like, here's what we can do." He sat up and leaned over his desk as if sharing a secret with me.

"Enroll in an interpreter training program. In the meantime, we will put you on the call list for interpreting jobs that would be appropriate for your skills."

"Interpreter training?"

"Yes, do you know about these programs?"

"Not really," I confessed.

He spent the next few minutes highlighting the different reasons interpreter training was beneficial, including ethics, environmental settings, and linguistics. After he finished, I expressed my appreciation for his time and headed back home.

I took Dr. Clearing's advice and enrolled at Harper Community College. I took the sign language placement test and was placed into ASL level five, out of five. After I completed this class, I would be eligible to take even higher level classes that would further polish my signing skills.

Level five was fun. It focused more on the descriptive styling of analyzing and retelling. On the first day, everyone in the class was asked to introduce themselves. We were aligned in a half-circle facing our teacher. She was Deaf and the only form of communication for the class was sign language. I was anxious, mostly because I hadn't been signing regularly for over six months. Each student introduced themselves and gave a reason why they were in the course. I was seated to introduce myself last. So far, I was feeling pretty good because I could easily understand everyone. One by one each student timidly went to the front of the class. I met Beth who had always liked sign language but wasn't seeking to be an interpreter. I met John; he wanted to be an interpreter because it seemed like fun. As we went down the line, I was feeling pretty good about my receptive skills. And then, a short stocky girl about five years younger than me walked to the front of the class. She rapidly signed, MY-NAME IS-J-A-N-E. But as she signed, my heart sank. This was what I feared; I wouldn't understand everything I saw. She utilized both of her hands like a presentation of synchronized swimming. Her arms were tautly extended and her movement stern and rigid.

She signed "MY," both palms coming to her chest. I thought maybe she was nervous, because I used only one hand to communicate "MY." She moved into the next sign, but her arms jolted forward. Her shoulders moved as if she was competing in the breaststroke. "NAME," both of her hands formed the word. The first two fingers extended, the rest folded. This looked right to me, but when she brought them together, she shook them both up and down. I always thought one hand was to remain still, while the other hand gently tapped the top of the fingers in a cross fashion. Hers were moving out and in and there wasn't a stationary hand. My heart filled with horror. Was I losing it? As if choreographed, she continued to the next word, "IS." I typically never signed "IS." Most times it wasn't needed, but with introductions I understood why all the students were using it. The sign for IS starts by signing the letter "I" by making a fist, extending the pinky finger out. The hand is then placed under the chin with the thumb towards the throat so the pinky finger is snug on the chin. The movement is two-fold. Extend the fist forward and bring the thumb to the front of the fist, which creates the letter "S."

But Jane was using both hands simultaneously, as if they were images of each other. She finished off her name with vigor. As she signed the first letter of her name J, with her right hand and held the bottom of her wrist with her left hand. Did it hurt her from all the extensive movements she had just made? No, she was presenting her next letter. Next was the A, anger seemed to form in her movements; N blared on her fingers loudly and then the letter E. I slouched. Jane paused before she continued her story: she graduated with a degree in sign language and Deaf studies and wanted to become an interpreter. Every sign was mirrored with her opposite hand. I thought I was seeing double.

I was so thrown off by her skills that I thought it was my problem. Had I been away too long? I began to doubt myself. The teacher took her place at the front of the room after thanking Jane for her introduction.

"I'll have to get used to your signing," she declared.

Immediately, I sat up, relieved that it wasn't just me. I hadn't lost my first language after all. When it was my turn to introduce myself, I walked to the front of the class and smoothly spelled my name. I told the class that my reason for being there was to become an interpreter. Looking back now, I know that was the intent, but I can't remember feeling any passion for it.

I really enjoyed the class. One homework assignment had us describe the layout of our homes. I was fascinated by the imagery the teacher displayed in her examples. She signed the entire hallway that led to her bedroom, even the lace doily on the table under a crystal lamp. It felt as though I was in her home. I became excited. This to me was performance art. I practiced and tweaked the placement and movement of my hands in order to aid others to visualize my apartment. This challenged me and renewed my enthusiasm to delve deeper into the language of signing.

I enrolled in American Sign Language Linguistics. To my surprise, I learned there were ASL rules. There were classifiers just as in English. ASL classifiers showed movement, location, and placement. I had had no idea the complexity of my native language. I also realized my thoughts were predominately in sign language. When I wrote, words came out in an order that was half English and half ASL. When I listened to lectures or seminars that weren't stimulating enough in English, I mentally broke down the words I heard and put them in sign language order. When I tried to express myself in English and could not find the words, my mind stopped in mid-thought. I needed to sign out the word. The English words were clogged in my brain but once I signed my thought, I could continue speaking in English. I discovered this also worked the other way around as well. When I was in the middle of signing, I would pause, speak aloud, and unclog my mental stopper.

Like the time at work, when I was required to attend mandatory work meetings on safety. To keep me interested and stimulated, I would take each sentence and mentally sign the concept. I imagined what signs I would use to capture the content. Sign language is a visual language and I needed something visual that helped me retain the information.

Linguistics was hard. I found my interest weakening. Homework was participating in Deaf events to report how I interacted and utilized my signing skills. This was when I started to make new Deaf friends in the Chicago area. The other students complained about the homework. It offended me. How else could they improve their signing if they didn't use it in a "real-world" setting? I became disgusted.

I dropped out of Linguistics and eventually the interpreting program. It became clear to me I didn't have the heart for it. Once again, I quit.

Both

THE SAME, YET DIFFERENT

I attended my first CODA conference in 1996 which was held in the Los Angeles area. I figured if I didn't like it, I could skip it and explore California.

The woman behind the registration table said, "We've been expecting you." It was a nice thing to say, and I immediately felt welcomed.

At the age of 23, I still had a strong desire to fit in, somewhere. Especially since all my life, people commented on how I was "different." Was that a good thing or a bad thing for a girl wanting to fit in? It would be decades before I figured that out.

As I navigated my way around the conference the first day, I couldn't believe all these people had Deaf parents. The opening ceremonies blended the spoken word with sign language. This confused me because I thought every one here was hearing. I enjoyed seeing my native language everywhere. Though I hadn't been there twenty four hours, I started to feel a sense of camaraderie. The commonality of all these people being able to understand my upbringing was overwhelming. I felt as though I could meet and talk to anyone, and he or she would "get-it." I began to let my guard down. It took me a few hours to change the way I talked to hearing people who had no connection to Deafness. In the hearing world, if I felt comfortable enough to share with someone information about myself, I usually revealed that my parents were Deaf. Here I found myself saying it right after I introduced myself. However, this was the last place I needed to do so.

I did this with a woman named Diana Nelson, who said, "How horrible!" She took a sip from her glass of white wine garnished with olives. Then she laughed. It was her way of poking fun at what I had heard for most of my childhood whenever a hearing adult learned of my parents Deafness. She winked and then added, "Can they drive?" Diana made me feel comfortable. She was able to make light of the stereotypes that hearing people had about Deaf individuals. The fact is that some Deaf driver's safety records are far superior to hearing drivers. Driving safe is almost totally dependent on visual awareness and alertness. Noise levels in certain circumstances can render hearing totally insignificant as a safety factor. Deaf drivers navigate visually, just as all drivers should.

Diana too had to endure these kinds of questions in her life. After meeting and talking to her, I was ready to fully immerse myself into the conference.

The next day consisted of breakout sessions and workshops. Since a large majority of attendees were sign language interpreters, several workshops enabled them to get continuing education credits. I skimmed the different categories of breakouts and saw some labeled vaguely such as "20-Somethings." There were breakouts on family dynamics like an OCODA (an only child with Deaf parents), and OHCODAS (only hearing child in their family but has Deaf siblings and Deaf parents). There were other breakouts that allowed reflection and grief support for those whose parents passed. There was one called "Fire and Ice," for hot topics that needed cooling down. I never went to this session, I imagined it had something to do with resentment.

I also learned there were different ways to spell coda. The organization itself wanted to be recognized as CODA, while those that preferred to be identified as part of the culture were Codas. Similar to the way Deaf and deaf were spelled. Many Codas would say the CODA conference was their Deaf Club, since they were in fact not Deaf, but felt Deaf culturally.

I attended my first breakout, "20-Somethings," without any expectations. When it was my turn to tell a personal experience, I shared my story of the prank telephone call. It was the first time I ever told anyone, let alone a roomful of people. To my amazement, I finally realized that I must have been harboring it deep inside. I didn't even know I needed to share it and once I did, it felt good.

Another participant shared a story related to using the telephone. It was nothing like my story; the only similarity was that it was something that happened on the telephone. As each one related his or her own personal experience as a Coda, I felt the bond grow stronger among my new friends. After the breakout, I approached the other telephone story person. I thanked them for sharing their story. I was relieved that my embarrassment was finally set free. But the person said, "Oh, my story wasn't as bad as yours," and walked out of the room.

My guard went back up.

I had thought this would be a place where people could help me. I had gone through life unable to find who I was, what I stood for, or even what my own likes and dislikes were. Since childhood I pursued a life based on what other people thought I should do. Whether they verbally told me (like my grandmother wanting me to be a lawyer) or what I assumed they wanted (like playing basketball because it was a visual sport). I did whatever they wanted and denied my true self.

I went back to my hotel room and sobbed. I realized there were hot tears of anger and cool tears of peace. That day in Los Angeles, my tears spilled a lukewarm, not angry and still not at peace. I wanted clarity so desperately. Despite the unintentional offensive comment, I thought I had found people just like me, finally. We were the same. To me "same" translated to "connected." It also felt as if it validated our similar experiences. The sign for "same" begins with the "y" in sign language. It's the identical hand shape used for telephone. The pinky finger and thumb extended, all the other fingers folded in. Beginning with the thumb about three inches from the heart, the pinky pointed outward. The movement—push the arm and hand forward about a foot away from the body. Stop, for a slight pause and then pull back, repeat. That slight pause visualized the support. It's the way the hand comes to another and pulls them close. For example, I enjoyed movies. SAME. The lights in my home flashed when the phone rang. SAME. I had to interpret school conferences. SAME. I was bullied. SAME.

There at the CODA conference, I wanted to feel the SAME. Looking back, because of my desperation to fit in, I jumped at assuming we were all the same. Since they all had Deaf parents, we must be alike. I would discover I was the same, yet different.

After returning home to Chicago, I was overwhelmed with the reality that hundreds of people had had similar experiences and backgrounds as me. Right there, I was surrounded by people I could talk to and could perhaps even help me discover who I was.

This actually frightened me. Why did I need another bunch of people to help me find myself? I wondered if it was a sign of weakness.

Hence, I avoided the CODA conference for three years.

In 1999 the conference was held in Australia; one of my lifelong dreams had been to visit Australia. Luckily at the time, I was a travel agent, another job I thought I would try after realizing being a paralegal wasn't for me. I worked diligently on an exciting pre- and post- CODA conference group tour to Australia. I knew I'd get free perks for organizing a group, which would ensure making my dream a reality. I successfully organized a group of 20. Now I was forced with a dilemma. How could I organize a group tour to the CODA conference and not go myself?

Although still weary, I decided to attend. I didn't want to call attention to myself for not being involved. I thought others were watching my every move.

This international conference was smaller and had a quaint feeling. I attended what I considered a safer breakout, Women's Spirituality. The facilitator was versed in meditation and relaxation. Afterwards, the facilitator said good bye to me and added, "You seem locked." I recoiled. I was not locked!

However, in retrospect, I realized, I had been locked for years, unable to find what it was about Coda that frightened me.

With each session and each Coda I met, I searched for the meaning of life in my own way. There were Codas who were professional interpreters. I wanted to know if they enjoyed it. I wanted to know if I had chosen the wrong path or if I should re-think becoming an interpreter. I met people who were involved in their Deaf communities. I found out about jobs I never knew existed, mostly because I had never been exposed to the fact there were teachers for Deaf students and others who worked in social services for the Deaf. I wanted to know about each Coda's relationship with their parents and how they felt about their childhood.

What started out as my need for self-discovery only ended up adding to my confusion. For some reason, I now felt I had to prove myself to another and new set of peers—the Coda community. My journey for self-awareness suddenly stopped.

I had another obstacle. My parents were not fond of the idea of Coda. Granted, they had no idea what it meant. They had formed their opinions from a distance. It became just another topic that I couldn't discuss with my family on the already short list of permitted topics.

I dipped my toe into the Coda circle and then pulled it out; it felt like a hokey pokey dance. I did get involved at the local level for a few years, and for a short time I served as the President of Illinois CODA. While I tried to educated others about Illinois CODA, I also wanted hearing people, Deaf people (whether they were parents or not), and other Codas to know about this unique sub-culture that existed among members of the Deaf community. My personal agenda was to educate Deaf parents about their hearing children. I wanted healthy conversations to start about what it's like for a child to be the conduit between two worlds.

As technology improved, I thought the work for a hearing child would lessen. But I learned that it could be just as frustrating as what my generation experienced. One younger child of Deaf parents told me that with automated phone calls, relay operators had difficulty connecting the phones due to the time constraints of pressing a number to get to the right department. This resulted in getting the call disconnected automatically. What I also found overwhelming were the kids themselves. I was being introduced to well-balanced, confident kids who were just awesome. These kids did get similar questions that I had growing up, like, "Can your parents read Braille?" and "How did you learn to talk?" But now, I met a new generation of parents who took advantage of educational opportunities. They acknowledged there were obstacles or differences that Deaf parents and hearing children may experience. Just because a child was born hearing to Deaf parents, didn't equate that they were "normal" like the hearing world. I was delighted to get to know these parents and their children. The wall I had built around myself was slowly crumbling. I took more pride when someone asked about my culture or the abilities of Deaf people I knew.

At the same time, I was exposed to a phrase from Coda peers I had never heard before: "Stupid hearing people." The phrase was used in a way to set up a vent. It was a flippant kind of comment, an insult that hearing people didn't "get-it." Admittedly, I even adapted to and used it, perhaps to fit in. However, it started to grate on my nerves. Even though I've had some mean and hurtful things said to me, I had never categorized people. For me, the "stupid hearing people" in my life taught me many things. I vowed to keep the phrase out of my own vocabulary. When I did, I saw people in a new way. I began to see people more than whether they were Deaf or hearing. While I thought I wasn't prejudice, I realized it was a form of compartmentalizing. It was not a Deaf or hearing thing. It was human thing.

I've attended seven conferences since 1996, each time learning something new about myself. The meaning of Coda for me finally changed. I permitted myself to live in and enjoy both the hearing world and the Deaf world. My journey with Coda showed me that I should embrace both worlds at the same time, with equal pride. It had nothing to do with another Coda's experience. It dawned on me that my life experience had taught me many lessons.

And that's when my real life adventure began.

CARL

In November 1996, some Deaf friends invited me to the Galaxy Bar in Des Plaines, a northwest suburb of Chicago. Every month there was a Deaf social meet up. When I entered the bar, I took a quick look around to find my friends. After seeing them seated at a high top table, I joined them. As I settled in, I couldn't help thinking none of these people were my parents' age. I also noticed that they were not only younger, but some of the guys were CUTE! I was in a new world. I learned new slang and jokes. I felt more alive with my expressions. My interactions changed. This wasn't like talking to my parents' friends.

The crowd at the bar began to grow, and I was introduced to more of my friends' friends. I mingled about and I noticed a boy across the room, leaning against the wall, staring at me. This was not unusual; for years people gawked at my signed conversations. I was used to it. I almost commented to my friend but decided against it. As we chatted, my friend made eye contact with the onlooker. The onlooker walked over to our table. I tried to figure out if he was Deaf. I decided to focus on the important things: his nice build, goatee and small swagger as he walked our way. He then turned to me. "Hi," he waved.

I waved back, a wave being universal really, to Deaf and hearing.

Then his hands and fingers went to work. "My. Name. C-A-R-L," he signed.

My eyes took in all I could at once. My first thought was, "This guy is hot." My second thought was, "He speaks my native language."

For the next few hours, Carl and I signed about motorcycles, Chicago, and our jobs. I learned he had a BMW bike, grew up in the suburbs, and was a carpenter. We played pool and flirted. We exchanged phone numbers, but I had to explain that I didn't have a TTY and would have to rely on relay operators. He told me he understood.

When it was time for me to go, Carl gave me a hug, and I embraced the nice build I had noticed earlier.

I bounced all the way to my car.

During the next couple of months, Carl and I had a few relay discussions. They were incredibly time consuming, and it was awkward to have a relay operator carry out our conversations. There was the long process to connect the call. The relay operator would announce, "Hello. This is Illinois operator 6658994. A person is calling you that is hearing impaired. Have you received a relay call before?"

After I responded, "Yes," the operator explained that she had to let the hearing impaired caller know the call was being connected. This sometimes took as long as seven minutes.

Each typed line the operator relayed for Carl took another five minutes. A simple, "How are you?" took at least two minutes. When I spoke there was an excruciating time lapse as I listened to the tapping of the keys. It was distracting having Carl communicate to me through a female operator who had a thick Mexican accent.

Our interest in continued phone calls eventually dwindled.

Then in January, a friend lent me his TTY, a portable model the size of a typewriter. My first call was to Carl. It was a Sunday. I dialed his number on my black and white Con-Air phone and placed it on the cradle of the machine. The number rang, and I could hear the squeaky squeals of Morse code transmitting words onto my screen. The digital font displayed and glowed in all capital letters.

I saw the words HELLO GA.

I typed HI CARL ITS ME LIYSA ...SURPRISE I GOT A TTY GA.

WOW....HELLO....GREAT GA he replied.

The conversation went on as I typed YES JUST WANTED TO LET YOU KNOW YOU CAN CALL ME DIRECTLY NOW GA

HOW ARE YOU QQ GA

The double Qs replaced the question mark symbol. It was quicker than shifting and finding the symbol.

My palms began to sweat. The difference between having a direct

TTY call and the labored relay calls was like a dream.

I'M FINE....HOW ARE YOU QQ GA my mind raced as I tried to find something interesting to say.

Carl typed back I'M FINE AND GLAD YOU GOT A TTY... THAT IS GREAT GA

I nodded. Trying to come up with something else to type. YES GREAT GA.

With my elbows propped on the desk, I twirled my finger through my hair and wondered how long this was going to last. I was trying to get to know him, but so far all we had said was HELLO and GREAT. I was so hoping the conversations would pick up now that we had a direct connection.

As I waited for him to reply, I got up and grabbed a glass of water from the kitchen. When I returned the message read WOULD YOU LIKE TO GO OUT ON A DATE GA.

I excitedly dropped the glass on the desk. I didn't realize how low the desk was and it crashed on the surface. Drops of water flew out onto the desk. Without sitting down, I typed SURE GA. My mind jumped ahead to figure out if I had any plans for the weekend.

HOW ABOUT TODAY? GA.

I sat down. I pumped my legs up and down. My toes started tapping.

GREAT I typed. Again, I wished I had more to say. I added I'LL COME BY YOU GA.

We finished up with directions, and I told him I'd be out in a couple of hours.

Our first date began with dinner at Dave & Busters, and we then went back to Carl's house to watch a movie, Mrs. Winterborne. Our date wasn't much different from the other dates I had. There were the same feelings of awkwardness when trying to get to know someone. At the end of the night as I got ready to go home, Carl walked me to the back door. My car was parked just steps away. He leaned in for a kiss and my body felt a nervous tingle. My eyes wouldn't close. I psychoanalyzed each of his moves. My mind squealed, "I'm about to kiss a Deaf guy! I never knew there were Deaf people my age!" As our lips touched, I allowed myself to melt. I felt the kiss and fell into his arms.

Carl and I had started our relationship quickly. I knew he was in the process of a divorce, was set to be finalized in a few months. He also had a son, age five. We had only been dating for six weeks before he asked me to move in with him.

I did.

GENERATION GAP

When I started dating Carl, I was pleased he would be able to communicate freely with my parents. I was relieved that I wouldn't have to translate. But, when I brought him to meet my parents for the first time, there was tension. Dad's body was stiff as a board. My mother was somewhat reserved. Conversations were artificial. I felt awkward in my own parents' home. It was probably nerves, I thought.

Actually, before meeting me, Carl knew who my father was from past bowling tournaments. Dad had co-chaired the 1994 Detroit tournament of the Great Lakes Deaf Bowling Association and Carl had seen him there. They had not officially met, however.

We struggled to make conversation and Dad grew increasingly odd. He got up from the chair and went into the kitchen. He returned with a bottle of water and sat down. Two minutes later, he got up again.

Carl, meanwhile was tuned into the football game. Mom was in the kitchen checking on the casserole. When Dad came back into the TV room, I waved to get his attention.

I signed, "What's wrong?"

My father sat down on the couch. He hung his head down. He swayed it from side to side, as if he was going to say "no."

I knew this gesture. I knew it from the moment he hung his head down.

I had seen it when I could not play hockey. I had seen it when I could not take the promotion at the mall. I had seen it when I moved to

Chicago. It was the signal that he was about to object.

My heart pounded.

The side-to-side movement of his head was usually followed by a slow sigh that emerged into a low rumble of an engine about to turn over.

"Ummmmm, I'mmm not happy," he voiced, not using his hands.

I forced myself to sit still.

His hands started to sign, but they fell into his lap.

My eyes jetted over to Carl, who was still focused on the football game. The Detroit Lions were losing to the Chicago Bears.

"Not happy?" I signed. I leaned forward. "Everything ok?"

Like a bottle cap exploding from built-up air, Dad's hands bolted up. "You. Him. Not. Happy," he said. His hands flashed faster than a squad car's lights.

I couldn't imagine what it was he didn't like about Carl and me.

I tried to recall previous conversations. What didn't he like? Carl and I had been dating for three months. How could this be?

"Not. Happy," he repeated.

"But I am happy," I replied.

He looked through me.

"You. Not. Happy. We. Live. Together?" I asked. The sign for together is two fists coming together side-by-side, fingers touching, thumbs extended to depict two people, collectively.

"No!" he snapped his index and middle finger crushing into his thumb. His voice boomed like a cannon.

My mind raced. Living together didn't bother Dad. Was he mad that Carl was going through a divorce? Had a child? Was older by five years?

By this time, Carl had seen glimpses of the conversation, but not all of what had happened. He sensed something. "What's wrong?" he asked.

My eyes filled with tears. "Time. Go," I said.

I urged Carl to leave with me while Dad repeated, "Wait! I. Not. Happy." Now he signed and spoke.

"Dad. I. Not. Know. Why. You. Upset!" I knew from the moment he said he wasn't happy, there was going to be a judgment against me. I tried to remain calm and to get Carl to leave without an explanation. I was standing. Carl was not. I again said, "Let's go—now."

I turned to get my coat. Dad blurted out in an exerted grunt, "No hearing and Deaf date."

I closed my eyes. I needed a moment to register what I had heard. My father had just called me. . . hearing.

My father repeated, "No hearing and Deaf date." His breath rode low in his chest resulting in a sustained sound.

Carl looked confused. The combination that I was rushing him to leave and my father wasn't signing everything resulted in his confusion.

Later that night, Carl told me that I looked shocked and was actually shaking at this point in the argument with Dad.

I had stood in my parent's home stunned. My mind kept repeating hearing, hearing. He had called me hearing. Growing up, "hearing" was made in reference to the outside world of our home. "Hearing" was the word that ignited disappointment, rage, and confusion for my father. He never trusted anyone "hearing." Hearing people were the crux of his problems. They ignored him, taunted him, and took advantage of him. They disrespected him.

And, they isolated him.

And now, he viewed me as hearing. Was this the undercurrent in our push-pull relationship? There was love, but there was loss too, for both of us. I felt this from my fingers to my toes.

I looked over to Carl. I tried to fill him in, but things were happening so fast. I forgot to sign. I couldn't articulate, due to the shock and anger inside me. My heart ached for Carl because he was being left out of the conversation and therefore he couldn't respond. He didn't even know what the hell had just happened. I remember thinking how ironic that Dad having been isolated during his life was now the offender.

Carl and I finally managed to get our coats and started to leave. My father followed us out the back door. Carl and I exited the house and went through the swinging gate of the chain link fence that ran the length of the driveway. We walked down the driveway to the car. Dad followed on his side of the fence. He waved to get Carl's attention.

Carl stopped. He faced my Dad. The fence separated them.

Dad signed, "Daughter. Not. Good. For. You. Go. Find. Someone. Better!"

Carl took a minute. He tried to sign back, but Dad's signs were still hanging in the air. When Carl started to reply, Dad cut him off.

"You. Deaf. Go. With. Deaf."

My jaw dropped.

"My. Daughter. Not. Deaf," he said.

Carl replied with "Naw," raising his hand as if swatting away the idea in mid air. Then with his hands smoothing the air and his head tilted to one side, he added, "I love her."

Carl and I married three years later, in 2000.

Over time I realized that Dad and Mom were from a different generation of Deaf in a hearing world. They went to Deaf schools. All of their friends were Deaf and it was with them that they felt most comfortable.

Carl, on the other hand, went to a Deaf program in a hearing school and later was mainstreamed with Deaf and hearing children. He attended the same school and the same classes as hearing children. The Americans with Disabilities Act included equal access and educational opportunities for all.

Carl also had many hearing friends. Each of them communicated in their own way, using home signs, or made-up gestures.

My mother once told me, "Carl's not like us."

No, he's not. In fact, Carl and I joke that I'm more Deaf than he. I was raised by Deaf people who taught me the habits of stomping my foot on the floor, flicking light switches, and pounding on a table to get someone's attention. Carl, raised by hearing people, never learned foot stomping or hand pounding.

I don't think my parents realized, while they were raising a hearing daughter, they were also nurturing my Deaf heart.

WHY I'M NOT AN INTERPRETER

After learning about the interpreting profession, I still struggled with becoming an interpreter, especially when asked, "Why aren't you an interpreter?"

My parents' friends assumed I already was an interpreter. "Where do you interpret?" they asked. When I told them I'm not an interpreter, they replied, "Why not? You. So. Good. Signer. I. Thought. You. Deaf."

When Deaf people commented that they thought I was Deaf, this ignited my pride. Since I had loved to see myself sign, practiced and thought in sign language, being validated by someone Deaf always made me feel accepted.

Many hearing peers asked, "Why aren't you an interpreter?"

I said, "Not interested."

"But you're so good," they responded.

For years, I would go back and forth. Should I interpret or not? I had already tried it and quit. I knew that in order to become an interpreter, I would need formal training.

Illinois passed a law making it mandatory for professional interpreters to have a license. I still thought about it. Even in 2005 when my family moved to Wisconsin, I contemplated pursuing it as a career. It wasn't until 2008 when I finally realized WHY I didn't want to be an interpreter.

In the small Wisconsin town called Two Rivers, Deaf friends were vacationing. They had a minor fender bender and texted me, asking to come and help. Police were already on the scene. I made my way over there in less than ten minutes.

I hadn't done this for anyone else in a really long time. I had translated for my husband, but our interactions were so connected. For example, if we were at the bank, I could nod and he'd understand it meant, "The shares of your stock have dwindled and inflation has risen, the housing market is crumbling, and your FICO scores indicate you don't have many options."

If I had declined to help my friend with their fender bender, it would have taken hours to find a professional interpreter. We did not live in a very Deaf populated area. I wasn't really thinking about it, I just opened my heart, grabbed my keys and took off to meet them. When I arrived at the scene, my friends were there along with two police officers, and the other driver. I introduced myself as I walked up to the group. An overwhelming sensation swept over me. I was extremely nervous. When I get nervous, I like to crack jokes, but I didn't want to make the situation worse for my friends, so I didn't say much.

Not only was I nervous, I felt an amazing need to do a good job. Generally, for a non-injury vehicle accident, I wouldn't have been nervous around a police officer. But, I wanted to brief the police officer in Deaf culture. I wanted him to understand there was going to be a delay in communication as I translated; I wanted him to know I knew how to sign really well, just as all those hearing people told me I could. I wanted to articulate beautifully the signs into spoken words.

Stress weighed on me and I feared I might not be able to speak or sign.

We walked down the block to the site of the incident. My friend explained how he had pulled out of the parking space, and the other driver side swiped him.

As I was translating the sign language, all I could think was, choose the right words Liysa, choose the right words!

I wanted to make it adamantly clear that it was not my friend's fault. I could not fail my friend. The police officer went from talking to us to the other driver, and then to his partner. My stomach was in knots. I felt like my fingers wanted to detach from my hands. I squeezed and cracked my knuckles.

The entire situation lasted about thirty minutes. My friend was found to be in the right, and the other driver was issued a ticket. My body relaxed as if a rhinoceros had just gotten off of me. I was shaking.

I said my good-byes to my friends. They thanked me, and I drove home.

During my drive home, I couldn't figure out why I was so uncomfortable. In a moment of clarity, I felt it. I had become too emotionally involved. Growing up, I put an extreme amount of pressure on myself. I wanted my parents to sound eloquent. I felt the need to deliver clear wise word choices hoping everyone would think my parents were as smart as I knew they were. I also never let on when I heard an English word I didn't understand. I listened to the entire sentence and tried to figure out any foreign vocabulary. I feared my word choices for my parents' signs would come off as choppy and uneducated. I didn't want anyone to form impressions of my parents that were not true. I wanted my parents to be viewed as well as I could make them because it was my voice the hearing people heard. It was my voice hearing people responded to, not Mom and Dad's signs.

I was afraid of how I would feel while hired to interpret situations that would remind me of my childhood. It would be a doctor's visit, an educational setting or an insurance seminar that would spin my emotion into anxiety. I was afraid of feeling my childhood all over again.

I also felt strongly that Deaf people were oppressed. I was far too biased. It was as if the Deaf person needed to win.

Like the time in 1978, there was a softball tournament in Chicago, hosted by Central Athletic Association for the Deaf. Mom, Dad, Marty and I stayed at my parents' friend's place in Chicago and I remember being awed by the housing so close together and the hustle and bustle of a big city. In the morning, Dad drove south on Lakeshore Drive to Grant park, they had a dozen baseball fields. My brother and I were in the back of the car.

A police siren started up. I looked around; it was behind us. Dad saw it in his rearview mirror before I could tap him. Dad merged onto the shoulder. As the police officer came to the window, my dad sat straight up. I was so nervous. I waited until I was cued from Dad to come to the front of the car. The police man arrived at the window and immediately started talking. My dad pointed to his ear and shook his head side to side as he tried to relay "cannot hear."

Dad waved me up to my post, which was hanging over the front seat to his right. The officer explained that Dad was swerving in between lanes.

I told Dad, "You. Drive. Swerve."

While facing the police officer, Dad immediately said, "Sorry." He then looked at me, "Tell 'em, I was talking to my wife and I didn't realize. I'm sorry."

I tried to formulate the words and then told the officer, "My Dad says he's sorry. He said. . .he was talking to my Mom."

Inside I was scared. It sounded too simple. I didn't want Dad to get in trouble with the police. I envisioned the police officer misunderstanding me, ordering Dad out of the car, cuffing him and hauling him off to jail.

I pressured myself to make sure he wasn't going to be in trouble.

The officer looked at me and then looked at my Dad. His head nodded.

"OK, tell your Dad, I'm going to let him off with a warning but please be careful."

I was relieved.

As I drove back from Two Rivers, a bit shaken from a minor fender bender I wasn't even involved with, the light bulb came on: clarity does not come in the form of what you want or think you want. It comes in the form of what you do not want. At that moment, I clearly no longer wanted or needed the responsibility of signing. I did not need signing to define me. What I needed was to define myself.

⟮ RAISE THE ROOF

In 1990 when I started college, my brother Marty was still at home. It was my hope that he would handle my parent's interpreting needs. By then, technology had emerged and the new device for Deaf people was the fax, which enabled my parents to communicate with the outside world. For example, they could now schedule their own appointments and carry on conversations with their friends. It was quicker than using the TTY and significantly faster than the Relay. Mom would write a note and fax it to her friend. She would finish the laundry as she waited for a reply. Sometimes, if she knew her friend was waiting on the receiving line, she stood and waited. The back and forth of the fax messages predated instant messaging. In the meantime, our parents relied on us less and less to interpret for them. Another result, or at least a coincidence, was that now Marty and I rarely talked to each other.

He remained a bachelor and I started a family. When he did visit, he drove all the way from Detroit to Chicago but only stayed a couple of hours and then went home. We seemed to have nothing in common.

Then years passed and Marty's life changed. He married and became a father of two. His commitment to teach his children sign language was notable. He at last discovered the world I had known for many years, both as a child and now as a mother. He investigated sign language and dug deeper into many of the benefits of having a bilingual child.

During a Thanksgiving visit, Marty and I talked kids. At the time, my nephew was 14 months old. We talked about the cute laugh he had, the eyes that sparkled and about how fast babies grow. While I was sitting in a chair in Marty's family room, and holding my little nephew, Marty paced. He was excited, nervous and tired as were most new fathers. He started up a conversation.

"So yeah, my little man can sign *milk* now."

"That's great!" I said, as I looked at the baby in my arms.

"Yeah, I mean, this is new to me. I know you have your girls signing already."

"It's so fun. You'll see how much they respond as you continue to teach them."

"I'm so excited that he can communicate with me."

I smiled. I found holding the baby to be very relaxing.

"Yeah, and I know you know ALL about this."

I nodded. I thought he meant, signing to my kids.

"You've always been into this," he continued.

My attention broke away from my nephew's adorable face, and I turned to look at Marty. He had stopped pacing.

"Huh?"

"You were always into this."

"I'm not sure what you mean."

"You know," His tone shifted.

I didn't know. "What are you talking about? What am *I* . . . into?"

He half-smiled. "The Deaf thing," he said. "You were always interpreting."

"Yes, that's true. You were too lazy."

For a moment the word lazy seemed to catch him off guard, but he continued.

"I mean, you married a Deaf guy."

"I thought you liked Carl."

"I do."

"Then . . . then . . . then, what?"

"Then, he's Deaf."

"Sometimes I wonder if you are, too."

"You married a Deaf guy."

"You already said that."

"You were always involved with the Deaf stuff."

"WHAT are you talking about?"

"You liked to interpret."

"I had to interpret."

"Well, you liked it."

"I don't think I had a choice."

"Well, I'm just saying, you were always interpreting. You married a Deaf guy, and you got involved with Deaf things."

I felt a shooting pain across my forehead. It never occurred to me he thought I married someone who was Deaf because I was *into* the Deaf thing.

I realized he had no idea who I was and I had no idea who he was, even though we had lived under the same roof for eighteen years. He had no idea what I stood for, what my thoughts were, or that I didn't think Deaf/hearing was a black/white thing. I longed to run home to Carl, the man who loved me, who just happened to be Deaf. My brain searched to find some kind of heavy-hitting insult. I always became defensive too quickly. I didn't want to argue anymore. I looked into his son's eyes and found the peace I needed, the serenity that comes with holding a child.

"You have Deaf parents too," I said, suddenly and surprisingly calm.

"It's not the same."

I didn't know it at the time, but he was right. It was not the same. It started to become so evident to me, that although we lived under the same roof, Marty and I had a different upbringing with different responsibilities.

The strengths of my responsibilities led me to be a strong, independent person. I was able to get things done for others easily. I became a problem solver, sort of. The biggest problem I had yet to solve was, who am I? I had walked around with this question for years. I kept asking it over and over. But, it was the wrong question.

I should not have been asking, who am I? I should have been asking, who do I want to be?

WHAT'S MISSING?

After that visit with my brother, I reflected more. I couldn't help but feel there was still something significant about my life I needed to uncover. I asked myself was there something dynamic missing from my childhood? Was it something in my parents or in me? At first I thought it was love. I thought maybe they didn't love me in the way I needed. But I wasn't sure what that might have been. Upon future reflections, however, I realized they demonstrated their love for me in so many ways.

Under our roof, we were a small family of four. Marty and I had chores; emptying the dishwasher, dusting, and vacuuming. They taught us to share in the workload. We also had bedtime curfews and we needed to ask for permission to have friends over.

There were celebrations including several birthday parties. My birthday is in July. I remember Mom and Dad organizing my fifth birthday. They called me in from playing with a neighbor. I was wearing my pink one piece swimsuit because I was playing in the sprinkler. I entered through the back door and walked into the kitchen. A large doll house was displayed on the table, the same table on which I would later discuss life insurance as I interpreted for my parents.

On my seventh birthday, Grandma Lill and Grandpa Bill drove in from Kentucky. This party was held in the basement with my friends from school. It was a green-and-yellow theme and there were plastic ballerinas dancing on my cake.

My Sweet 16 party was a surprise. I drove home with a friend from the mall, only to find our two car garage loaded with streamers, balloons and pictures of me. The garage was filled with my family, my friends, and Mom and Dad's friends. So, if all of this was good, what was missing?

Mom and Dad went on to create even more magical moments. During Christmas time our house was full of the colorful lights of the season. For a long time, Mom even decorated two trees and every year there were plenty of presents. One year everything was wrapped in silver foil paper. Every present!

As I recalled all the wonderful things they did for Marty and me, I still couldn't place the void in my life that I felt.

Several times we went to Kentucky to spend the holidays with Grandpa and Grandma. My grandparents' house had two living spaces. Upstairs there were bedrooms along with a family room and kitchen. The daily activities took place downstairs where there was a family room, kitchen and small bathroom. The couch had a pull out bed and I slept there during our visits. One year, I was sick and lay snuggled up on the couch. It was Christmas Eve and my family was eating dinner in the downstairs kitchen. All of a sudden, I heard a noise. I looked over to the kitchen table where everyone was seated. Marty and I made eye contact.

A few moments later, there was another sound, and my Mom looked at me. "What's wrong?"

"Bells, I hear bells," I said. I scurried off the couch but Dad ran in front of me and told me to wait. He had to check if the coast was clear. When he motioned for me to come up the stairs, I flew up them three steps at a time right past him to the Christmas tree. There were presents everywhere. It was a miracle.

Now as an adult and mother, I don't know how they afforded it all.

Their love of traveling resulted in lifelong memories. There was the time during a charter fishing excursion that I puked my guts out. I was leaning over the side of the boat. Marty scooted alongside of me and asked, "What are you looking at, whoa. . .oh, no." A few days later on the ferry to Newfoundland, our ship sloshed about in the ocean so hard that the waves rose over the portholes. I puked again.

Even in my adult life, they never stopped showing me their affection and love. After I got married in Lake Tahoe, they threw a reception for Carl and me back in Michigan to share the joy with their friends and our extended family. When my children were born, they hosted baby showers and traveled to visit. I watched them as they tried to learn how to gently hold a baby all over again.

I struggled to find myself as I got older and our relationship was strained many times. I was still trying to find myself and still be Mom and Dad's child. The strain caused arguments, hurt, and confusion, mostly with Dad. We're so much alike, I saw this more and more as I got older. Not just in characteristics, but in expression. Dad could only show what he learned. His mother demonstrated little interest in his life along with being unable to communicate and better understand his needs. I could see the same pattern in our relationship.

Several times, Mom told me, "Your Dad loves you." I wasn't sure why she shared that with me. Perhaps she knew it was something I needed to hear. Maybe she intuitively wanted to explain Dad's capacity to love.

I never questioned his love for me. Even if I had, I was reminded of Dad's love at Marty's wedding reception. After dinner, I was eager to mingle with my parents' friends, the people I had know my entire life and that were a part of my childhood. We said hellos with hugs. As I look at them with my adult eyes, I saw how they had aged. They asked about my family and I shared small conversation about my life. They told me about their own children, the ones I remembered playing with at softball tournaments, bowling alleys and in the D.A.D. Club coat room.

My father was standing next to me, watching. He turned to me during a break in a conversation. He spoke and signed at the same time, "Your. Signing. So. Beautiful." I saw the emphasis. It took form when he closed his eyes and slightly bowed his head in respect. His fingers opened wider in a slowed movement as his knees bent with a slight genuflection. I remember I slightly exhaled, my heart flipped in my chest. A beam of light illuminated my soul. It all felt as if Dad was validating my love for sign language and for a moment, he didn't see me as hearing, but as his daughter.

Yes, my parents loved me. But, did they know I loved them?

As a young child I was always willing and ready to be there for my parents. I wanted to help them. I knew they needed me. I navigated complex situations and obtained the most information possible for Mom and Dad. When the doctor wanted to leave the examination room before all of our concerns were addressed, I managed to stall with several more questions I asked on my own. If I noticed that the communication between someone from the hearing world and Mom and Dad was uncomfortable, I'd flip to moderator role to ensure each party understood. If I thought my questions would bring me more clarity of how to translate the important information, I asserted myself to become educated on the topic at hand.

I was delighted to provide for them. But, had Mom and Dad viewed my childhood chore as providing? As love? I believed it to be love.

If there was love, then what was missing?

As I dug deeper into my soul, I became frustrated. Trying to grasp the concept and type it in English failed me.

I lifted my fingers from the keyboard. I closed my eyes. I mentally sifted through my life timeline, grasping for what was missing. Thoughts took hold of my hands.

My memory returned to elementary school. The hurtful insults that pained me, the insults my parents never heard. Insults I heard about them and about me. I had carried the insults for all of us. I absorbed the pain for them.

The sign for pain is two index fingers pointing at each other; mostly it means to hurt. When placed in the area of pain, my heart, my fingers were aimed at either side of my heart, and then, to add to the pain, I felt each wrist rotate as far as they could. A twisted heart pain.

My hands and heart beat faster. My memory returned to that horrible prank call so many years ago. Neither, Mom or Dad ever learned of the line of questioning. They never heard the tone in my voice and the uneasy responses. They'd never know the embarrassment I felt. How could they? The sign for embarrassment is similar to hiding behind your hands; no one can see me. To add to it, the hands repeat an up-and-down movement, showing humiliation over and over.

My fears, anger, and sorrow flowed from my heart to my hands. I kept asking myself, what more do you want? At first, I thought I wanted them to protect me. But, their love for me did provide protection. And then I saw, they protected me as only Deaf parents could.

With that, I looked inside my heart. What I was missing wasn't something someone else could provide. What I was missing was that I didn't believe in myself. I was strong and bold on the outside, but inside I was a mess. I couldn't make a decision without asking for several different opinions. And even then, I would try to choose the opinion that would lead to the greatest approval of me.

This kind of lifestyle drained me. I saw my pattern of jumping from school to school and job to job. I thought I would be defined by my degree or paycheck. When I acknowledged this, I wept cool tears of peace.

Fear next crept in with the breakthrough of having to turn my life right-side up. After years of operating one way, which those around me were accustomed to, I was now changing. I began to have more faith and trust in myself. The moment I embraced that, I felt a shift. I began to feel liberated. I was finally able to release the judgment I had over myself. This was now becoming an exciting part of my journey. I couldn't wait to see it unfold.

AFTERWORD

In 2010, I set out to write my own affirmation. I needed to create an inside balance that was positive and confident, just like how I performed on the outside. I needed to demonstrate what made me happy, something I had denied myself in the past.

When I thought about what made me happy—what I wanted to do—I recalled a vision I had never let go. I remembered standing outside my high school auditorium, looking at the stage and imagining myself on it, light illuminating my hair, my peers applauding in the audience. With that, I decided to create and write my own one-woman show. I called it *codadiva* and launched it in March 2011. I purposely did not capitalize *codadiva* because my personality now felt capitalized, so the title did not have to be. In preparing the script, I connected with old classmates from elementary to high school and was stunned to discover, most did not know my parents were Deaf. I had had the impression that everyone knew. I had thought I was living in a fishbowl with all eyes on my every move.

Perhaps all along, I had been on stage, acting, disguising both of my worlds. I had been one person, performing two characters.

After each *codadiva* performance, people approached me to share how they had related. These were people with no connection to Deafness. Their feedback showed me my gift was my voice. Indeed, I had been the voice of my parents for so long, I didn't know if I had one of my own. I didn't even know what it could sound like. On stage,

I found it. It was a voice that was clear and compassionate. A voice that rose up and turned heartache on its ear. A voice that galvanized support for bilingual and bicultural people. A voice that bore witness to difficulty and transcended it. A voice with power and resilience to tell women and especially girls, everywhere—never give up.